TARGETING NARCO-SUBMARINE NETWORKS THROUGH DEEP PENETRATION, AUTONOMOUS MARITIME IRREGULAR WARFARE UNITS OPERATING WITHIN A HUNTER-KILLER ROLE

A Master Thesis

Submitted to the Faculty

of

American Military University

by

R.J. Godlewski

In Partial Fulfillment of the

Requirements for the Degree

of

Master of Arts

August 2013

American Military University

Charles Town, WV

NOTICE: Insofar as possible, this thesis has been kept as close to the original submission as permissible. However, for matters of economics and expediency, certain aspects – such as illustrations – have been printed in grayscale while other formatting issues have been ignored due to printing alterations.

ISBN-13: 978-1499760958

ISBN-10: 1499760957

The author hereby grants the American Public University System the right to display these contents for educational purposes.

The author assumes total responsibility for meeting the requirements set by United States copyright law for the inclusion of any materials that are not the author's creation or in the public domain.

DEDICATION

To Sara (07/25/1951 to 12/13/2003), my love; Joseph (11/29/1918 to 04/14/2008), my father; and Theresa, my mother. Truly the first to believe in my capabilities.

ACKNOWLEDGEMENTS

I wish to thank the faculty of American Military University for their guidance and support throughout the years, especially Professors David Woodworth, David A. Morris, Scott Swanson, William Gawthrop, Steven Greer, and Paul Gelpi.

ABSTRACT OF THE THESIS

TARGETING NARCO-SUBMARINE NETWORKS THROUGH DEEP PENETRATION,
AUTONOMOUS MARITIME IRREGULAR WARFARE UNITS OPERATING WITHIN A
HUNTER-KILLER ROLE

by

R.J. Godlewski

American Public University System, May 16, 2013

Charles Town, West Virginia

In virtually any armed conflict, there remains an individual or individuals who cannot – or will not – surrender to capture by legitimate public authority. Recognizing this reality, this study explores the need for targeted killing of key personnel engaged within the design and construction of undersea craft employed by Latin American cartels to smuggle illicit narcotics and other contraband towards the United States. Using network analysis, empirical judgment, structured debate, and analysis of competing hypotheses, this study concludes that present American strategy vis a vis the Colombian cartels has failed to stem the flow of drugs towards the U.S. and that targeted killing of key personnel engaged within the narco-submarine networks represents the paradigm shift required to regain strategic advantage in the war on drugs.

TABLE OF CONTENTS

LIST OF TABLES

LIST OF FIGURES

I. INTRODUCTION.

In 1969, U.S. President Richard M. Nixon declared a prominent "war on drugs," implying a sincere intent to undertake any effort possible to reduce the amount of illicit narcotics affecting his nation. Twenty years later, by the end of the 1980s, President Ronald Reagan declared illegal narcotics to represent a clear and present danger to American society and formulated a broad strategy to combat the growing menace of drug producers and traffickers.[1] This menace soon involved the likes of Colombian Pablo Escobar, a notorious cocaine kingpin and indiscriminate murderer whose downing of a commercial Avianca airliner in November 1989 earned the infamous "narco terrorist" an American classification as a legitimate "military target".[2] The eventual killing of Escobar by the Colombian police "Search Bloc" a few years later, however, did little to cease the rising flow of narcotics and other contraband northward towards the United States from South America. The subsequent threat evolved into a sinister collaboration of various drug cartels[*] and paramilitary/guerrilla groups such as *Fuerzas Armadas Revolucionarias de Colombia* (FARC).[3] The U.S. war against drugs now bore a legitimate, militarized adversary determined to circumvent American sovereignty through any means necessary.

In prosecuting this war against illicit, "recreational" narcotics, especially that involving the cocaine trade originating from within Colombia, the United States faces two fundamental challenges. First, the U.S. encounters an adversary that, unlike perhaps Islamic jihadists, will not readily succumb to either death or incarceration. They seek to thrive and survive through escape and evasion. Secondly, the U.S. confronts a clandestine transportation network that excels at developing advanced smuggling technologies, particularly that involving submersible maritime vessels, to elude the detection of even the most sophisticated military and intelligence assets. These challenges conspire to offer American

---

[*] Some researchers suggest that the term 'cartel' represents a regrettable misappropriation of verbiage, "sacrificing conceptual and empirical clarity for stylistic convention". See Kenney, "The Architecture of Drug Trafficking", 233. Nevertheless, this study continues to employ the term for convenience, as most readers assume the definition to represent a coordinated criminal group seeking to profit from broad narcotics production and distribution.

military and law enforcement agencies an adversary broad in its capabilities and extremely resilient in tactics. Furthermore, the Colombian narcotics cartels remain shielded beneath an ability to corrupt and subvert indigenous counterdrug resources, hindering local cooperation with American personnel. At best, U.S. efforts team with Colombian federal police forces to investigate narco-submarine construction sites via the noise of insertion by helicopters or riverine vessels, betraying the arrival of counternarcotics units. At worst, American efforts remain sabotaged by subversive participants fueled largely through bribes and coercion. Whichever problem manifests itself, U.S. efforts remain telegraphed widely to the cartel counterintelligence networks, defeating the secrecy of counternarcotics operations undertaken by American personnel.

To defeat this poisonous enemy requires that the United States reevaluate its covert campaign against those *individuals* supporting and controlling fundamental nodes of the cocaine transportation network, particularly that involving emerging trafficking technologies. Foremost amongst these efforts must be the direct targeting of the social networks providing the development, construction, finance, and operation of undersea vessels that do provide transport of cocaine and other contraband beneath the waves, far beyond the scrutiny of legitimate international naval forces.[4] These vessels range from towed "cargo torpedoes" on through Self-Propelled, Semi-Submersible (SPSS) and Self-Propelled Fully Submersible (SPFS) vessels capable of carrying several tons of cocaine for thousands of miles during each voyage.[5] This study addresses the subsequent question; *will the growing sophistication of undersea craft employed by the cartels force the United States to target these threats before they exit the confines of indigenous waters for the safety of the open sea?* Specifically, the study introduces the hypothesis that *the U.S. will seek to asymmetrically target* specific individuals *to prevent the construction and/or launching of undersea craft carrying contraband towards the United States.*

From here, the assumption emerges that the U.S. will have to employ divergent, covert, autonomous (freed from micromanagement) units performing long-term reconnaissance, surveillance, and intelligence (ISR) of prospective targets before engaging within a hunter-killer capacity to neutralize such threats. Present U.S. counternarcotics operations remain necessarily classified and quite beyond the analysis of private, independent research. However, several avenues of research remain available owing to the presence of official military doctrine, historical case studies, and empirical presumptions. These options provide an opportunity to gauge current U.S. practices via open-source information and validate, for instance, the propensity of American-Colombian counterdrug operations for employing massive, thunderous deployments telegraphing movements to adversarial forces. From here, research will suggest that the United States' policy towards illicit narcotics has done very little to stem the flow of drugs into America and therefore a paradigm shift in military offensive procedures are warranted.

II. LITERATURE REVIEW.

Literature regarding cartel maritime trafficking vessels and the U.S. response to their emerging threat remains both broad and diverse, ranging from scholarly, peer-reviewed publications to popular works intended to steer public imagination. Amongst the more specific documents includes Lance J. Watkins' graduate thesis *Self-Propelled Semi-Submersibles: the Next Great Threat to Regional Security and Stability* conducted under the auspices of the Naval Postgraduate School.[6] This work provides a sound analysis of the subsea threat posed by Latin American drug cartels and its implications for regional and global security. Watkins' thesis serves as a solid foundation for those unfamiliar with the existence, or implications, of illicit undersea craft and their trafficking potential. Its primary weakness lies within its lack of suggestions for defeating such undersea cartel vessels outside the prospects for fortuitous discovery and interdiction.

Dr. Robert Spalding's book, *Drug Subs: the Worldwide Invasion by the Narco-Submarine Fleet* hints at a broader overview of the threat, yet fails somewhat in focusing upon the subject matter.[7] Despite apparent deception, many aspects of this book provide a critical overview of the potentialities

11

of global, illicit submarine networks shattering international sovereignties. Again, this represents yet another text or document identifying the problem but failing to formulate an effective strategy of extermination. It suggests a realm of 'look' but do not 'prevent' common to less scholarly works prepared for public and political consumption. Invading submarines, by definition, represent a critical disregard for national sovereignty and, therefore, warrant military countermeasures taken against their presence.

Less threat-specific represents Molly Dunigan et al, *Characterizing and Exploring the Implications of Maritime Irregular Warfare,* which considers the maritime irregular warfare (MIW) environment from the historical perspective in Vietnam on through current operations in Asia, Africa, and Latin America. The second "strategic scenario" within this book deals exclusively with counternarcotics and counterterrorism operations in Colombia, highlighting the concerns over SPSS technologies.[8] Despite being comparatively brief, the value of this RAND Corporation analysis rests with the book's covering of legal, technical, and operational considerations of narcotics submarines within MIW applications. This remains important for this study, for MIW operations and SPSS/SPFS vessels represent two key aspects of the base hypothesis. Its primary limitation being that, thus far, no researcher has taken the further step of intensifying MIW actions to defeat SPSS/SPFS construction and support operations.

Another RAND Corporation report, *Arms Trafficking and Colombia*, by Kim Cragin and Bruce Hoffman abdicates in favor of the generic arms trade serving guerrilla and paramilitary forces in Colombia. This report focuses primarily upon the smuggling of small arms, but the interconnection between legitimate arms for nation-states and the illicit trade bear scrutiny as the cartels do not remain afraid to accept weapons from any available source. H. John Poole's more popular *Tequila Junction: 4th-Generation Counterinsurgency* shares the hypothesis of employing small, combined action platoon (CAP) units to disrupt the terrestrial drug trade in Colombia. Poole's thesis rests with 'bottom up' counternarcotics operations that similarly represent a paradigm shift over current, more bureaucratic U.S. military operations.[9] Although not necessarily discussing either subsea vessels or the littoral environments directly, Poole's book supports, in practice, the very foundation of this particular study.

Shifting from tactics and technologies, Michael L. Gross examines the morality and ethics of targeted killings, the key assumptions made during the search for literature supporting the study's hypothesis.[10] These remain of paramount importance, for the legal issues involved within the study remain complex and very opinionated. His implication that individuals may be targeted because of mere association rather than bearing uniforms remains a key ethical consideration. Gross's book also encapsulates literature regarding international treaty, ethical norms, and common sense to centralize the issue of combating "dirty wars" while maintaining the moral high road. This is very similar to Thomas B. Hunter's self-published *Targeted Killing: Self-Defense, Preemption, and the War on Terrorism* that separates targeted killings from less ethical assassinations. Both books isolate a rather taboo subject within a manner that remains realistic, if not openly supported by the international community.

For its role, the U.S. Government (USG) tends to approach MIW operations within the riverine environment through several military manuals available to researchers largely through independent publishers. These manuals remain heavy on doctrine and very light on tactics or techniques. Such manuals remain "more about obeying doctrine than adjusting to ongoing circumstances" that represents the status quo within jungle environments dominated by asymmetrical drug trafficking organizations (DTO).[11] For the purposes of the study, these U.S. field manuals provide what DTOs defending their illicit operations in Latin America can expect from U.S. military operations. That is, these documents are undoubtedly read by those cartels seeking to circumvent American tactics, actually providing the DTOs with asymmetrical advantage over legitimate counternarcotics operations. Further literature can now be referenced thematically, building towards the ultimate concerns engaged by this study.

The World of Illicit Narcotics.

The use of narcotics by human individuals for psychological benefits certainly predates recorded history; Gregory D. Lee acknowledges that the first recorded use of cocaine by the Incas dates back some 2000 years.[12] These ancient peoples, through chance discovery and experimentation, understood that the consumption of certain plants and substances altered the human mind. Scholars have long written about the use of such hallucinogens to boost the warrior spirit within such ancient civilizations as the Aztecs in old Mexico.[13] Others, such as Paul Rexton Kan, declare that modern, irregular military groups often employ illicit narcotics as rewards for fighting as well as a means to stimulate atrocities against civilian populations.[14] More pursuant to this study, Kan writes, "…in Colombia, many combatants smoke basuco which is cocaine paste combined with marijuana and tobacco."[15] Further adding, "[m]ost telling about the use of *basuco* by Colombian guerrillas is that no one smokes paste except those involved in cocaine production."[16] Additional literature suggests that the war *against* illicit narcotics also *involves* drugs as a viable tool of battle.

Since the 1980s, FARC embraced the illicit narcotics economy as a fundamental means of financing its rebellion against legitimate Colombian authority.[17] This reality permitted the U.S. and Colombia to institute Plan Colombia (PC), which, amongst other provisions, sought to deprive FARC of "crucial operating income derived from the drug trade."[18] This indicates that both scholarly and governmental literature acknowledged the profound tactical and strategic influence of illicit narcotics' finances within asymmetrical conflicts. Other scholars, writing essentially for the popular market, direct more attention to introducing the actual production of cocaine, an essential consideration for combating trafficking technologies, as a means of communicating the broader challenge of illicit narcotics vis a vis American society and welfare.[19] Even HSBC, one of the largest banking firms in the world, had been fined for $1.9 *Billion* to escape being indicted in the United States for laundering drug money.[20] Such forfeitures, as that assigned against HSBC, suggest that "drug money" bears a significant influence over politics, international diplomacy, public safety, and capital enterprise, making it extremely difficult to isolate legitimate business from illicit opportunity.

Rachel Ehrenfeld, coining the phrase "narco-terrorism", arguably represents the world's foremost expert on the subject of illicit narcotics-fueled terror. Writing in *Funding Evil: How Terrorism is Financed – and How to Stop It*, Ehrenfeld provides a connection between Islamist-based Hezbollah ("Party of God") and Latin American training camps teaching children and teenagers the fine art of small arms combat.[21] More importantly, however, rests the assertion that *La Violencia*, the notoriously brutal period in Colombia that claimed several hundred thousand lives within the decade following the Second World War, merely transformed into lawlessness inspired by cocaine production and distribution.[22] From here, most scholars and security professionals acquiesce to the omnipresence of cocaine and other narcotics within Latin America and diversify their literary pursuits to analyzing the spread of drugs throughout the world.

The Intricate Network of Trafficking.

The literature regarding the production and transportation networks of cocaine and other Latin American-produced narcotics comes primarily from two different perspectives. First, scholars such as Michael Kenney tend to outline and address the *architecture* of narcotics smuggling, taking great pains to diagram the intrinsic nature of associations throughout any trafficking enterprise.[23] Others, writing from perhaps a more empirical perspective, concentrate on a more casuistical approach, often vilifying or condemning governmental agencies and associated military operations. Almost immediately upon the conclusion of the Vietnam conflict, journalists and other researchers charged the U.S. Central Intelligence Agency (CIA) itself with drug trafficking and other deviant practices involving illicit narcotics usage.[24] Such allegations, continuing until the present through such

15

television shows as History International's *America's Book of Secrets*, taint objective research into the implications of U.S. involvement within trafficking operations.[25]

This study will concentrate on the former approach; that of examining the architecture of cocaine smuggling as such a perspective sheds biases against those involved. Relying upon the concept of technology and its human, social apparatus provides researchers with an ability to cast aside discriminatory finger pointing. Methods of transporting illicit narcotics northward range from human mules, high-powered "go fast" boats, private and commercial aircraft (though advances in airborne technology have largely diminished this practice), yachts, fishing trawlers, cargo vessels, SPSS/SPFS subsea craft, and even today the appearance of autonomous undersea robotic devices.[26] The interviews conducted by researchers Decker and Chapman illustrate the vast repertoire of drug smuggling mechanisms available to the cartels and others profiting from the transportation of contraband.[27] What remains particularly noteworthy regarding this research is that the "cartels" possess a broad fluid dynamic, a hierarchy even more apparitional in nature than that involving Islamic Jihadists operating under the inspiration of al-Qaeda.

While many researchers have identified the presence of Russian involvement within the design and construction of modern, narco-vessels such as the SPSS and SPFS fleet, others such as R. Evan Ellis have written extensively about Chinese military involvement within Latin America.[28] This literature raises the question of Beijing's intentions within a region largely devoid of practical exports beyond narcotics and basic foodstuffs. H. John Poole, perhaps bearing the most military experience of the consulted researchers, itemizes Chinese purchases of land and facilities throughout Central America, suggesting the primary interest of the communist country in obtaining influence throughout a region erupting in sporadic bouts of Marxist/Maoist revolutionaries.[29] Given the nature of current literature, the personification of narcotics cartels as individually controlled criminal syndicates leaves much to be desired. What exists in reality, to the contrary, remain vast military conglomerates bearing infantry, air corps, and now a "silent service" sporting advanced submarines and subsea robotics.

Kenney reports, "the social diffusion of [Colombian] criminal expertise extends beyond drug trafficking to other forms of organized delinquency."[30] Decker and Chapman concur: "research has shown that the structure of drug organizations in Colombia has evolved over the past twenty years", implying a significant movement away from previous hierarchies as "the cartels broke up" and subsequent "groups shared control over movement of drugs" as the perpetrators adjusted to the evolution in control.[31] Taken collectively, the literature available illuminates a broad criminal challenge towards the United States, one as much military in nature as criminal, as violent as it is innovative, and as wealthy as it is primitive. This threat possesses aircraft, small arms, *narcotanques*,[32] submarines, and an undeniable propensity to inflict the most horrendous horrors upon anyone standing within the way of their business.

The Law and the Lawless.

Literature regarding international law and diplomacy often rests as unnecessarily complicated or severely opinionated, hampering any research into combating entities devoid of legal appreciation. These problems magnify exponentially whenever the discussion turns to narcotics trafficking and drug smuggling submarines. The presence of "stateless vessels" and U.S. interdiction of these craft within international waters has fueled a seemingly unending debate over due process and criminal definition.[33] Supporting a broad extension of Congressional authority, the U.S. Eleventh Circuit ruled that the Drug Trafficking Vessel Interdiction Act (DTVIA) of 2008 was "not exclusively a drug trafficking statue" leading scholars to realize that the statue itself "criminal[ized] the act of operating a stateless vessel."[34] In short, barring Supreme Court challenges, the United States could now interdict and incarcerate *anyone* operating or occupying a vessel bearing no national registry. This suggests the contention that such vessels, bearing no legitimate national recognition, *remain illicit no matter where they exist.*

Other researchers, notably Watkins, have acknowledged, "undercover DEA [Drug Enforcement Administration] agents have managed to penetrate [SPSS] operations posing as crew."[35] Such literature hints at the broad capability of U.S. interdiction efforts as such undercover operations appear to broach the vagueness of DTVIA provisions.[36] In assuming practicality, what the U.S. Government states, is that it bears legitimate authority in seizing any "non-state" vessel *anywhere* in international waters. Ann Marie Brodarick discusses the evolution of American legislation to adapt to the escalation of narcotics trafficking technologies and the subsequent alteration of practice by the offending DTOs.[37] This suggests an encounter between two diametrically opposed entities, one seeking to expand its jurisdiction over all unclaimed waters and another seeking to circumvent this tactic through traditional business assumptions of expected losses and additional markets served by advanced logistics.

Such moral dilemmas and the lack of consideration thereof, form something of a paradox for combating asymmetrical threats.[38] The literature, however, fails to provide a distinct consensus on targeting SPSS/SPFS vessels and the social networks that conceive, construct, and operate them. Foremost amongst the world's problems, as identified within the literature, remains the failure to arrive at ratified definitions of transnational crimes and the effort required to subdue these transgressions. Illustrative of this, remains the problem of genocide as defined by the United Nations (UN).[39] Such declarations did not ensure that UN forces would cease the wanton slaughter of ~900,000 Rwandans, for when "the wholesale extermination of Tutsis got underway...the UN troops offered little resistance to the killers."[40]   Astute researchers, therefore, must consider the suggestion that even the largest international body in the world remains largely impotent when confronted with the abject evil of individuals and groups feeling superior to others. Accordingly, present international measures fail measurably in ceasing even minimalist atrocities and, therefore, open opportunities for alternative doctrine.

Special Threats, Special Actions.

Beginning with the U.S. debacle in Vietnam during the 1960s and 1970s, Western military doctrine began a slow, methodical shift away from what had previously been considered "conventional wisdom". Military strategists were quick to denounce Army Chief of Staff General George H. Decker's assertion that "any good soldier can handle guerrillas."[41] Modern literature began to suggest that U.S. military manuals failed to promote initiative amongst America's fighting force, instead preferring to saturate soldiers with ratified doctrine.[42] This remains problematic for several reasons. First, the absence of initiative prevents American soldiers from responding to threats that, due to necessity, often change practices and procedures on the fly. Secondly, reliance upon officially sanctioned doctrine stalls aggressive action as soldiers and Marines often defer to authority before acting against the threat. Fortunately, post-Vietnam-era practitioners perceived the military imbalance and authored literature quite dramatic in analysis.

William H. McRaven, widely reputed to represent America's foremost expert on special operations (SO), devoted an entire popular text to formulating a theory of special operations replete with case study analysis and specific discussion into the merits of legitimate, authenticated special operations forces (SOF).[43] McRaven's "Six Principles of Special Operations" provide a foundation for this study.[44] This approach in qualifying SO missions has subsequently been supported by academics such as Robert G. Spulak, Jr.[45] What emerges, therefore, from the consulted literature, remains that SOF require soldiers that are warriors in spirit, creative in function, and flexible in application.[46] These hypotheses are supported by other practitioners, such as Scott Wimberley, whose popular *Special Forces Guerrilla Warfare Manual* focus upon small unit tactics, such as that employed by narcotics cartels.[47] This literature, remaining widely available, suggests that threats remain far more knowledgeable than U.S. soldiers constricted to approved and bureaucratized military doctrine.

Other literature provides a more practical, empirical approach to special missions. Uniquely important to this study rests Thomas J. Cutler's historical *Brown Water, Black Berets*; a profound study into U.S. Navy riverine operations during the Vietnam War.[48] What makes this volume unique for this research remains its depiction of mother ships, riverine patrol craft, and supportive technologies that form the basis of this study's hypothesis.[49] Other literature focuses upon the personal narrative and, while not necessarily scholar in its reporting, offers a profound psychological analysis of individual troops and their adjustment to combative environments.[50] Such literature serves as a stalwart against sanitized government doctrine, fueling unabated accounts of life within the trenches of war. Some of this popular literature, fortuitously, features individuals employed by American Military University, perhaps adding a fair degree of authenticity to the subject matter as these sources remain personally known.[51] Regardless, the subjective literature from the other side of the asymmetrical equation remains conceivably more persuasive to the cartels and guerrillas inhabiting Latin America.

Revolution of Violence.

Practitioners of irregular conflicts, at least from the command and control perspective, represent "a highly literate crew."[52] Despite being somewhat singularly successful in their individual pursuits, notorious guerrilla leaders such as Mao Tse-tung[53], Ernesto "Che" Guevara[54], Carlos Marighella[55], and even journalist Robert Taber[56] authored tactical studies widely read by their supporters and admirers. Other groups, such as the Irish Republican Army (IRA), collectively, have penned manuals of revolutionary zeal, legitimizing violence through various perceived grievances.[57] Many of these groups surpass U.S. military capabilities because their soldiers, largely through the necessity of remaining "low tech" sappers, understand the inherent value of remaining close to nature with all of its tactical advantages.[58] Although well studied by liberal scholars, such literature often remains ignored as trivial and sophomoric by conservative military strategists within the West.

To ignore the capabilities of an adversary because of predilections betray a sense of mirror imaging – the act of allowing one's own estimations to cloud judgment of another. This fosters such sentiments as General Decker's personal observation that "any soldier" could manhandle a guerrilla born and bred within the combative environment and whose future often leaves very little to lose. This literature, therefore, remains very important within any estimations of narco-guerrilla operations as many within the Colombian trafficking cycle approximate those sappers confronted during conflicts in Vietnam, Afghanistan, Iraq, Philippines, and elsewhere. As simple individuals, these combatants cannot be expected to author tactical treatises of his or her own accord and must, therefore, subscribe to practical judgment developed over eons of human evolution. The literature of Mao, Guevara, Marighella, and the IRA remain dissimilar only in the actual environment of the combatant, representing Asian jungle, Latin American hills, and occupied urban centers respectively. Any astute scholar will possess little difficulty in transposing one theorem upon the other's situation.

Where some guerrilla entities, such as FARC, fail, rests with an inability to shore the group's counterintelligence (CI) functions to keep state authorities from attacking the rebels. Graham H. Turbiville, Jr., among other scholars, note that FARC has suffered from the loss of its old line advisors, such as Manuel Marulanda Vélez (succumbing to heart attack in 2008), and subsequent CI operations "began to fray visibly in the 21st century".[59] What this literature suggests, is that new FARC personnel have resorted to personal electronic technology to transmit messages. This violates longstanding practices (prominent in the East) of avoiding electronic communications in favor of guarded communiqués.[60] Such minor deviations portend a shift away from security towards convenience, a subject few other researchers have capitalized upon, perhaps mirror-imaging Western expectations upon the whole hemisphere. If validated, this trend supports the thesis as criminal

21

elements will likely move away from the primitive tactics required to gain asymmetrical advantage over U.S. forces.

III. METHODOLOGY.

This study approaches research from two different perspectives; that of identifying pertinent, comparative case studies that suggest a historical appreciation of efforts to defeat transnational criminal organizations (TCO) and empirical recommendations derived to fill the void left by the historical record. In the first method, a taxonomy of structured analytic techniques consulted involves Key Assumptions Check, Network Analysis, Scenarios Analysis, Analysis of Competing Hypotheses, and What If? Analysis, incorporating primary and secondary open source literature from the peer-reviewed and popular record. A determination will be made from what has been tried to cease contraband flowing towards the United States via subsea vessels along with what technology remains available to support these measures and, perhaps, improve their efficiency. In the second method, a more empirical approach is employed to authenticate expert judgment; a stochastic approach being made to diminish personal biases occurred whenever rendering opinion.

The dependent variable of this study remains the response of the United States to the growing threat of SPSS and SPFS vessels employed by Latin America narcotics cartels. The first independent variable represents the relative isolation of vessel construction sites. The second independent variable represents the classification of High Value Targets (HVT) representing vessel construction and/or operations personnel. The third independent variable represents the ability and will of the United States to launch autonomous military forces against cartel assets located in foreign locations. The fourth independent variable represents the influence of local governments by indigenous Latin American populations, particularly regarding outside foreign intervention.[61]

Theoretical Framework.

Several rather convenient assumptions are necessarily made within this study. First, it remains assumed that the 'war on drugs' enacted by President Richard M. Nixon in 1969 and largely acknowledged by subsequent administrations, represents a sincere desire by the United States to defeat illicit narcotics trafficking organizations as befitting any hostile invasion by nation state or non-state threats. This threat assumes the characteristic of a powerful weapon system (narcotics) supported by the availability of an equally powerful "fifth column" within the United States (the drug buyers).[62] Such a threat serves two distinct functions – funding hostile actions taken against the United States and its allies, and irreparably damaging American society from within.[63] A second assumption rests upon the complexity of the overall narcotics problem. As with the targeted killing of Pablo Escobar in 1993, "*Because there is no final problem definition, there is no definite solution*", meaning that the scope of this study rests upon the most current available information and particularly tight constraints of time.[64]

A broader assumption rests with the narcotics trafficking organizations and allied guerrilla groups themselves. That is, because profits from trafficking define the purpose, DTOs will adopt any innovation, enter into any association, and commit any atrocity to safeguard their mission.[65] DTOs, therefore, remain bound to no law but their own and recognize no national border or sovereignty. Because of the apparitional nature of narcotics production and smuggling operations, there remains virtually no consensus on whether the threat from these organizations represents a military or law enforcement problem. This lack of exclusivity contaminates any prospect of determining the legality of many proposals herein. For this reason alone, the assumption remains that discretionary targeting of narco submarine construction and support nodes represents a last resort effort undertaken by any U.S. administration.

The study will base itself upon a meta-analysis to synthesize expert judgment and structured analysis to determine the validity of covert 'false flag' operations[*] targeting narcotics cartel maritime engineering programs. Such analysis may or may not include evidentiary reasoning, historical method, case study method, and/or reasoning by analogy to reach its conclusions. Tactics and technologies will be extracted from the historical record as well as proposed from expected future capability to suggest efficient methods of engaging illicit subsea vessel operational networks. The Social Network Analysis Knowledge Exploitation (SNAKE) model[66] discussed by Scott Swanson will be consulted and modified into a model incorporating McRaven's relative superiority concept leading to an investigation regarding asymmetrical operations within the riverine jungle environment.

Research will consult data from legal, diplomatic, operational, environmental, and technological perspectives to formulate an argument based upon empirical judgment rather than ethical expectations alone. That is, consideration will focus upon the consequences of failing to act rather than hesitating to infringe upon diplomatic, legal, or social courtesy. Nevertheless, analysis will be isolated from biased data involving equipment, training, maneuvers, doctrine, and classification of personnel. The approach used will neither discriminate against nor effectively support non-U.S. doctrinal operations as the hypothesis suggests that local, "bottom up" techniques work more advantageously than traditional bureaucratic "top down" (e.g., micromanaged) missions that potentially handicap military/law enforcement operations against largely indiscriminate narcotics cartels and affiliated guerrilla and paramilitary forces.

Limitations.

Covert and clandestine operations against DTOs engaging within the subsea trafficking of narcotics and other contraband present a unique consideration for the United States and academic researchers contemplating solutions to the problem. The available sources remain classified and the

---

[*] For the purposes of this study, 'false flag' operations represent those missions where counternarcotics personnel pretend to represent cartel or criminal groups in order to specifically target those cartels and/or criminal groups.

public rarely receives word of any operation beyond the spectacularly successful. Few, if any, missions involving SPSSs are made known beyond specialized texts and a popular episode of a crime documentary or two. Because SPSSs and the devolution of narcotics "kingpins" to loosely aligned confederations, the existence of trafficking networks takes on a more sinister, if less dramatic, characteristic within the counternarcotics profession. Anything beyond drug treatment programs, aerial and maritime interdiction, and criminal prosecution rarely conjures up intense scrutiny from scholars. Many researchers conclude that the problem represents a psychological and sociological dilemma and therefore direct efforts at ceasing America's massive consumption of recreational drugs. Others hypothesize that the best solution rests upon a law enforcement approach where both providers and consumers receive broad penalties for his or her infractions.

Because of these rather simplistic approaches to an otherwise extraordinary problem, little research – or theory – exists on tackling a major node of the narcotics trafficking pipeline that could result within a significant diminishing of illicit drugs and contraband reaching the United States from Latin America. Scholars that resist martial thoughts equate with politicians who, perhaps, might reduce military capability out of fear of incurring collateral damage. The analogy remains valid for the fundamental reason that potential solutions are ignored because of potential problems. Until the research community considers *all available* hypotheses, little can produce dramatic progress one way or the other. Within a mathematical analysis, such determinations suggest that $A + B = C$ only if A and B represent tolerable (if not expected) values. This study functions upon the speculation of proper Presidential Finding authorizing covert military/paramilitary operations and an intense commitment from the U.S. Government, its various agencies and units, and members of Congress that subsea narcotics smuggling represents a clear and present danger to American national security and warrants few restrictions in the prosecution of the 'war against drugs'.

IV. FINDINGS AND ANALYSIS.

In early 2013, U.S. Southern Command (SOUTHCOM) admitted to ISR support for Central and South American nations that led to at least "32 high-value narco-terrorists killed in action."[67] Victor Suarez Rojas, commander of FARC forces, was himself killed in 2010 during a raid orchestrated by the Colombian military, suggesting that U.S. ISR involvement in counternarcotics operations in Colombia extend back several years.[68] Certainly, the Pablo Escobar affair culminating in the trafficking kingpin's 1993 death underscores the sincerity – and capabilities – of American involvement.[69] These actions further identify with the long-standing efforts of the U.S. 'war against drugs' and serve to dismiss further argument on whether or not U.S. administrations have taken an aggressive stance against narco-criminal enterprises secreted within foreign locations. Therefore, this study dismisses any subsequent consideration of U.S. intent to engage within activities that lead to lethal actions taken against DTOs and affiliated personnel in South America. Rather, the study focuses upon the merits of available tactics and technologies targeting these high-value targets (HVT) and the threats they produce.

The Threat.

Phil Williams, a leading expert on transnational criminal organizations, suggests, "a growing recognition that organized crime often operates through fluid networks rather than through more formal hierarchies."[70] Accordingly, these networks:

> …vary in size, shape, membership, cohesion, and purpose. Networks can be large or small, local or global, domestic or transnational, cohesive or diffuse, centrally directed or highly decentralized, purposeful or directionless. A specific network can be narrowly and tightly focused on one goal or broadly oriented toward many goals, and it can be either exclusive or encompassing in its membership.[71]

Williams continues:

> …when they are targeted by law enforcement, many criminal networks are inherently dispersed, with the result that they do not provide obvious centers of gravity or loci for law

enforcement attacks. Lacking a physical infrastructure or a large investment of sunk costs that would add significantly to their vulnerability, networks can also migrate easily from areas where risks from law enforcement are high to areas where the risks are much lower.[72]

This analysis confirms the suspicions of Decker and Chapman, whose contention remains that

Colombian drug trafficking organizations had begun relatively quickly to move away from

Figure 1. Areas under consideration. Colombia map: U.S. Central Intelligence Agency.

so-called cartels.[73] Kenney ascertains that this reality has led to the U.S. effort against narcotics trafficking basing itself upon "a fundamental misunderstanding of the Colombian drug trade", which is why this particular study began with a disclaimer revolving around the mere use of the term 'cartel'.[74] Swanson detects a parallel situation involving improvised explosive device (IED) social networks, "[t]he present IED social network tends to be comprised of very fluid, linear decentralized structures with a number of recurring roles."[75] These decentralized nodes of criminal networks make them extremely resistant to targeting and serve as a powerful 'business continuity' policy similar to that employed by legitimate business operations.

Fortunately, from time to time, even criminal networks must absorb traditional methods of operation to further their tasks. The use of aircraft, ships, and private conveyances employs conventional vehicles even if the underlying mission remains rather secretive and illicit. Unfortunately, the U.S. Government often fails to appreciate the concentration of such vulnerabilities. Watkins quotes the former Deputy Assistant Secretary of Defense under the George W. Bush Administration, Richard Douglas, in outlining the methods behind the United States' "three zones" of attacking SPSS vessels.[76] This tripartite approach rests upon attacking the source zone where narcotics are manufactured, the transit zones of the world where such products are trafficked, and finally the destinations where narcotics arrive.[77] Sadly, such policies illustrate an attack against apparitional targets, necessitating a very large commitment from American and indigenous forces. These measures search for the proverbial needle *after* it has safely reached the haystack, not before.

Combating illicit subsea craft, however, requires prudent search and discovery methods engaged long before such vessels can reach the safety of the open sea. In this regard, only the origin and termination of the vessel's operation remains effectively open to law enforcement and/or military interception. Beyond these points, the vessels represent a three-dimensional threat from which to appear and disappear nearly at will. At present, such submarine craft represent the apex of competitive

29

adaptation employed by the DTOs seeking to shield their trafficking operations from prying eyes.[78] This process tends "to select and retain practices and procedures that achieve satisfactory results, while…disregarding those that do not."[79] Illustrative of this, remains the shift away from airborne trafficking arrangements – which have largely been defeated through the use of U.S. Airborne Warning and Control Systems (AWACS) operations – towards maritime vessels, culminating with the employment of various low-profile vessels (LPV) and submersibles.[80]

Submersibles, in particular, seem to have caught the academic community by surprise. Decker and Chapman, for instance, believed that such vessels represented "the talk of myth rather than reality" and only acknowledged the existence of submerged vessels carrying narcotics (the solitary reference involving a capture in the Caribbean during 2007) through a deeply embedded endnote.[81] This contrasts with Watkins, who reports the existence of a large vessel discovered in 2000, bearing the potential of diving to "325ft (99m) and capable of carrying 10-15 tons of cocaine."[82] Perhaps more revealing, Dunigan et al report that "SPSSs may have hauled 423 metric tons of cocaine in 2008 alone" according to data extracted from the State Department in 2010.[83] Such capabilities represent a serious threat from a "myth". Another vessel, "discovered in February 2011, was large enough to carry eight tons of cocaine and four crew members in its air-conditioned interior and included a small kitchen."[84] Obviously, the threat from undersea narco vessels is evolving at an alarming rate.

The realization of narco-criminal networks and the emergence of submersible and submarine vessels underscore the complexity of Latin American drug trafficking as the broad, defuse social networks hint at a comprehensive construction and support environment largely shielded from international scrutiny. The sophistication of SPSSs can range from "homemade" to comparable with emerging navies, each operational for up to two weeks and 2,500 miles, and costing anywhere from $300,000 to $1,000,000 for models based upon Russian designs.[85] Such networks require designers, engineers, builders, financiers, sailors, captains, security personnel, and a range of labor to construct

30

and operate these vessels. It remains inconceivable that Colombians account for the entirety of the SPSS staff. Nor is it possible that the DTOs have escaped outside influence within their design and operation. With the potential for the illicit transportation of human cargo as well as weapons of mass destruction (WMD), the influence and participation of a broad range of nation-state and non-state entities conspire to complicate the SPSS/SPFS networks.

The Players.

The emergence of the first SPSS vessels after the collapse of the Soviet Union bear some scrutiny, as comparable studies involving the 'brain drain' from the Former Soviet Union (FSU) nations suggests that some 900,000 nuclear technicians and workers with moderate to high-level security clearances had departed Russia following the collapse of communism.[86] If even an arbitrarily low percentage, say 1%, of comparable defectors from the Russian submarine industry, a key partner for the nuclear field, were to seek incomes outside of their host nation, then the figure available to Colombian DTOs could conceivably approach ~9,000 individuals. Although it remains problematic to ascertain the precise number of ex-Russian submarine experts flooding the marketplace post-1991, the potentialities for even a few highly qualified engineers and designers to reach Colombia remains feasible. Watkins reports on the discovery of a SPSS outside of Bogota whose construction plans were written within Russian, suggesting the presence of not only a chief designer, but of Russian builders (or, at least, Russian-speaking Colombians) as well.[87]

Historically, Russia has been a significant military supplier and partner to Latin America, its influence exceeding the confines of the Cold War.[88] More recently, in 2006, there was an interest "in further military-technical cooperation between Colombia and Russia" with Russian Mi-17 helicopters being supplied to Colombia as earlier as 1996.[89] A greater dilemma rests with Russia's arms shipments to neighboring Venezuela that include "24 military planes (Su-30 fighter jets), helicopters (types Mi-35M and the Mi-26T), 100,000 AK-103 Kalashnikov rifles, 1000 *Dragunov* sniper rifles and *Igla* surface-to-air missiles (SAM)."[90] More importantly, the "fear is that these rifles could find their way into criminal hands or into, even worse for Colombia's military, the [FARC]."[91] Cragin and Hoffman report, "[w]eapons routinely move from Venezuela into Colombia", and that many of "those weapons are registered to the Venezuelan Armed Forces."[92] Compounding the Venezuela-to-FARC arms smuggling scenario rests a deal for the Western Hemisphere's first Kalashnikov factory to be constructed in Venezuela.[93]

FARC, for its role, had sacrificed its ideology in the 1980s to fund and expand its operations through illicit narcotics, soon "known to be involved with all areas of the drug trade including cultivation, production, and distribution."[94] This suggests a direct connection with the narcotics submarine vessels and, by extension, the prospects for a link between Venezuela and the illicit subsea fleet. FARC's immersion into the broader body criminal accelerated with the loss of several "old discipline" commanders that kept the guerrilla movement secure and operational.[95] This decline allowed several paramilitary organizations to push FARC out of the major urban centers and neighborhoods permitting the (ostensibly) right-wing groups to dominate civic efforts leading to a broadening of quasi-governmental networks throughout Colombia.[96] These actions serve to diminish the concept of legitimate public authority.

Another significant player within Colombian weapons and narcotics trafficking appears to be the People's Republic of China. Not only are the Chinese selling weapons to the FARC and other anti-Colombian groups, "a significant portion of the military-caliber weapons purchased by narcotrafficking organizations" as far away as Mexico "are Chinese in origin".[97] China is also beginning to flood Latin America with its version of the Colt M-4 carbine, the NORINCO CQ-M4.[98] Two of Colombia's neighbors, Venezuela and Ecuador, have purchased sizeable quantities of Chinese military hardware and at least one Venezuelan official, Amílcar Figueroa, "presented a shopping list of weapons for the FARC during his visit to" NORINCO in China.[99] Apparently, the Chinese *raison d'etre* in Latin America remains to gain as much influence – and currency – as possible. With Chinese-Latin American aerospace and naval cooperation a reality, it remains extremely plausible that narco submarine networks have benefitted from this omnipresence of Chinese military expertise as well.[100]

A presence in Latin America fits well with China's *guerre du peuple*, a cultural desire to manifest itself within the politics and militarism of a region.[101] Leftist ideologies, even from amongst certain Jesuit priests, in Colombia predates even the exploits of Pablo Escobar, leading to fertile soil for Beijing's recent manifestation within the region.[102] In fact, it has been argued, that the Asian and South American cultures bear much in common and that U.S. strategists often ignore the simultaneous involvement of drug traders, crime families, Islamic militants, and Maoist guerrillas within comparatively small regions.[103] While this observation generally constructs itself around South America as a whole, the four groups coalesce around the profitable illicit opportunities emerging in Colombia. As with Vietnam during the 1960s and 1970s, U.S. leadership often fails to recognize the most serious threat for all of the peripheral commotion.

American involvement within the drug war materialized rapidly with the exploits of Pablo Escobar, particularly the Colombian's downing of the Avianca airliner in 1989.[104] It represented this event in particular that led the George H.W. Bush Administration to conclude that Escobar represented a direct threat to American citizens beyond the mere production and distribution of cocaine northward.[105] The U.S. response, especially after Escobar "escaped" from self-incarceration, involved CIA and Delta Force special operators in addition to perennial DEA agents. Nevertheless, the U.S. approach to counternarcotics leaves much to be desired. It has more often than not, despite the intentions of the first Bush Administration to employ special operators and surveillance assets, persecuted the war on drugs as strictly a law enforcement matter.

Even when the American military is employed, chances remain that its soldiers function more according to hierarchal doctrine rather than tactical prowess.[106] Facing an adversary that innovates through necessity, perhaps one supported by an antagonistic nation-state such as China, the U.S. loses asymmetrical advantages by adhering to impractical counternarcotics techniques. This modern drive away from primal warfare remains, perhaps, unnatural, for the heritage of the American military heralds from expanding its frontier on through various deep penetration, special operations conducted in Laos during the Vietnam War and continues today with U.S. Navy SEALS [Seal, Air, Land commandos] operating within the Central Asian mountains of Afghanistan.[107] The 18th Century's development of Major Robert Rogers' "Rules of Ranging" could have been written specifically for today's counternarcotics units conducting missions in Latin America.[108] The precedence for aggressive, "tough as woodpecker lips" clandestine jungle warfare during Vietnam through the Studies and Observation Group (SOG) missions bears scrutiny vis a vis Colombian counternarcotics operations.[109]

With its rich history of close-quarters, low-tech infantry battles from the Revolutionary War on through the Plains Indians campaigns of 1865-1879 and onto the enduring struggle of Vietnam during the 20th century, the United States military *should* be well versed within the fight against TCOs, terrorists, and FARC guerrillas operating along the coast and riverine environments of Colombia. Nevertheless, the migration away from primeval warfare towards a more courteous, diplomatically accepted form of combat rests as a fundamental constituent of American political thought during the early 21st century. The preference today appears to concern itself with fewer casualties and more arrests than in the past. To understand this new manifestation of war, one must consider the legalities arising during the latter half of the 20th century and, particularly, the reemergence of 'ageless' asymmetrical warfare.

Table 1. Comparison of Military Cultures.

UNITED STATES	ASIA	FARC/NARCO-TCOs
Top down hierarchy	Bottom up networks	Loose networks
Established doctrine	Empirical reference	Capitalistic evolution
Technology-driven	Human-driven	Human-centric
Stand-off appreciation	Close-quarters combat	Close-quarters combat
Large unit operations	Small unit operations	Small unit operations
Improvisation by permission	Improvisation by choice	Improvisation by necessity
Special mission novelty	Special mission preference	Special mission opportunity

Of Law, Diplomacy, and Expected Norms of Behavior.

Dick Couch, in discussing the concept of moral conduct within warfare, states, "Tactical ethics, by my own definition, is the moral and ethical armor that accompanies our warriors into battle."[110] He writes of this following a short narrative in which he recounts hearing a witness tell of [presumably] U.S. Navy SEALS beating an Afghan prisoner "of little value" to death in northern Afghanistan.[111] This story epitomizes the difficulties experienced by the American soldier – how to fight barbaric wars without descending into barbarism. Michael L. Gross, writing within *Moral Dilemmas of Modern War: Torture, Assassination, and Blackmail in an Age of Asymmetric Conflict*, identifies severe beatings, maiming and mutilation, and sexual abuse as interrogation techniques among "those that everyone rejects".[112] Apparently, not all members of the U.S. armed forces agree to this rejection, which further explains the great difficulty inherent in corralling soldiers caught within the harsh realities of war.

At the other end of the spectrum, notorious drug groups such as the (now largely dissipated) *La Familia* cartel in Mexico were known to lob severed heads onto crowded dance floors to announce "divine justice" against those the group declared unworthy of life.[113] The issues rising from Abu Ghraib prison in Iraq, the Guantanamo Bay detention center in Cuba, and historical atrocities encountered by every military service on the planet create certain paranoia within those public figures duly bound to safeguard national reputations and integrity. Legitimate public authority, in considering the dilemma of international warfare, conspires to adjust between measures of military necessity and humanitarianism.[114] To understand the boundaries of permissible warfare, therefore, one must first analyze the existence of battle. In this regard, the study focuses upon those historical case studies that bear merit in considering the threat from narcotics groups operating independently within the riverine environment.

Case Study #1: The Plains Indians Conflicts (1865 to 1879).

Almost immediately upon the cessation of hostilities between the United States and the Southern Confederacy during the American Civil War, numerous conflicts erupted between the native population and settlers living within the western portions of the country. Thomas Goodrich outlines the problems associated with post-war American westward expansion and confrontation with the Plains Indians, where battle was often an "unpredictable, unending, and utterly unnerving [form of] war where the front line was very often as close as the next ravine."[115] The atrocities committed during these conflicts, by both sides, often involved the intentional murder – and even scalping – of innocent women and children.[116] The final key to success within this conflict, however, rested with the infusion of a "deepening insight into the Indian mind", a combination of massive force and "skilled diplomacy", and the employment of native scouts to combat native tribes.[117] Similar tactics remain valuable in countering narcotics organizations along the littoral.

If one can make the argument, as Goodrich implies, that American expansion into the western plains *forced* native tribes to fight back to protect their interests, then one can certainly argue that American consumption of narcotics "forces" Latin American DTOs to feed that demand and, accordingly, protection of their economic interests is expected. From this perspective, the U.S. delegitimizes its military actions. That is, the rationale for American defense fails under its pressure against indigenous peoples. Alternatively, one could also make the argument that attacks *against* Indians materialized in retaliation for attacks against soldiers defending peaceable settlers. In the words of one such American, "Twenty-one of our dead soldiers were lying on the ground, stripped naked and mangled in every conceivable way. I noticed one poor fellow with a wagon tire across his bowels, and from appearances, it had been heated red-hot and then laid upon him while still alive."[118]

It is easy to decipher the dilemma within the foregoing scenario and match it to today's operations against drug traffickers. Yes, perhaps the settlers (and American soldiers) should not have ventured out west into the Plains, but regardless of the progenitor, soldiers *are expected* to protect their country's citizens and fellow comrades in arms, especially from acts of extreme violence and atrocity. Juxtaposed into Latin America, the argument now becomes, "Yes, Americans should not consume illicit narcotics, but the United States *is expected* to protect its citizens from criminal acts of extreme violence and atrocity." Any group that *beheads* civilians, despite the location, becomes an enemy in the eyes of those who subscribe to this line of reasoning. The international rationale for this approach incorporates the concept of 'just war':

> The strict conditions for *legitimate defense by military force* require rigorous consideration. The gravity of such a decision makes it subject to rigorous conditions of moral legitimacy. At one and the same time:
> - ✓ the damage inflicted by the aggressor on the nation or community of nations must be lasting, grave, and certain;
> - ✓ all other means of putting an end to it must have been shown to be impractical or ineffective;
> - ✓ there must be serious prospects of success;
> - ✓ the use of arms must not produce evils and disorders graver than the evil to be eliminated. The power of modern means of destruction weighs very heavily in evaluating this condition.[119]

As with the Plains Indian Wars, the national perspective could argue that illicit narcotics flow from groups that will not cease irrespective of some Americans' willingness not to consume the drugs. Legitimacy here rests with, "The *use of drugs* inflicts very grave damage on human health and life. Their use, except on strictly therapeutic grounds, is a grave offense. Clandestine production of and trafficking in drugs are scandalous practices. They constitute direct co-operation in evil, since they encourage people to practices gravely contrary to the moral law."[120] Such indictments support the concept of just war outlined above. First, the acknowledgement exists that narcotics represent a grave threat to the human condition (first condition). Second, the reduction of drug use within the United States or, alternatively, the legalization of narcotics remains very much impractical and ineffective (second condition). What remains is that whatever military action eventually emerges, it must provide serious prospects of success and the use of arms must not produce disorders greater than the threat from the DTOs (third and fourth conditions).

The legacy of the Indian Wars rests with the condition that "[l]egimate defense can be not only a right but *a grave duty* [emphasis added] for someone responsible for another's life, the common good of the family or of the state."[121] Just war provisions aside, the United States Government during 1865 to 1879 found itself with the *grave duty* to protect its citizens and, arguably, conducted its Plains campaigns with as much effort to avoid emerging as a greater threat than the Indians were themselves. In consideration of the effort against DTOs and subsea trafficking vessels, the United States holds all of the qualifications of just war doctrine with the added advantage of receiving the invitation from the Government of Colombia (GOC) to participate within counternarcotics operations. Nevertheless, riverine warfare – because it constitutes recognition of national coastlines and sovereignty – bears a unique consideration as both intentionally and unintentionally trespassing upon others' borders. To evaluate these prospects, we must turn to another historical case study.

Case Study #2: U.S. Involvement in Vietnam, Cambodia, and Laos (1961 to 1975).

Wars throughout most of the Industrial Age centered upon declared conflicts, recognizing the boundaries of legitimate nations. Even during the massive world wars of the first half of the 20th century, the vast majority of the warring population who did not violate their sovereignty recognized neutral countries. Beginning in 1945, however, international conflicts shied away from the constraints of official declaration. Despite a brief three-year commitment to combating North Korean soldiers (and some intervening Chinese) during 1950 to 1953, the Vietnam War epitomized the United States' newfound fascination with conflict outside the protocols of Congressional – or international –

ratification. The conflict also represented a paradigm – if temporary – shift in how the U.S. population appreciated and staffed its military forces. The war in Vietnam represented a dichotomy between guerrilla/insurgency operations and conventional struggles, the latter defining the conflict following the notorious (and unsuccessful) Tet Offensive of 1968.

As Summers relates, paraphrasing former CIA director, William Colby, "Saigon did not fall to barefoot black-pajama-clad guerrillas. It fell to a 130,000-man 18-division invasion force supported by tank and artillery."[122] Despite this reality, however, America has forever been branded with having had lost a guerrilla campaign, despite its oft-ignored 192-year history of successfully waging *la petite guerre*. From the revolutionary war against Great Britain to the Civil War that saw countless examples of Southern units turning to ambushes and raids and onto the Chindits in World War II Asia and Philippine revolution following that conflict, American soldiers have been quick to improvise small unit tactics and abandon conventional wisdom to extract victory from the jaws of defeat. What Vietnam represented, eventually, remained a televised conflict in which borders were often ignored for tactical and strategic advantage. That is, even non-combatants within neutral countries could witness firsthand the shattering of national sovereignty by aggressors both large and small, both nation-state and non-state.

The notorious Ho Chi Minh Trail that permitted guerrillas (and other military units) to funnel personnel and supplies into South Vietnam diverted through Laos.[123] This forced the United States into either invading 'neutral' Laos to attack the communist supply lines – at great disadvantage under international security – or simply permitting an avowed enemy tactical and strategic advantage. Concerning another Vietnamese neighbor, Plaster states rather succinctly, "This American policy of downplaying, even denying, enemy violations of neutral Cambodia was simply without precedent."[124] Here rests an indication that the United States was hamstrung by either international diplomacy or domestic politics. Regardless, U.S. military forces *did* take measures against communist elements operating in both Laos and Cambodia. The precedence here is that the United States would not permit enemies safe haven within allegedly neutral countries, a trend that appears during the present involving remotely piloted vehicles (RPV, or colloquially known as 'drones') attacks in Pakistan.

The situation in Southeast Asia bears scrutiny in consideration of present and future conflicts. First, the United States entered into a massive, long duration war without the clarity of a formal declaration of hostilities.[125] This led to not only confusion during the crisis, but ambiguity long afterwards.[126] Secondly, the United States, in fighting a determined, asymmetrical adversary, found itself expanding this war into neighboring countries. This suggests a further dilution of national boundaries in relation to modern wars and underscores the present conflict against Islamic jihadists and narcotics groups – nations may respect borders but criminal organizations will not. Mao hints at this problem, writing in regards to previous Chinese conflicts of the late 18th and early 20th centuries, "…the fact that victory was not gained was not because of any lack in guerrilla activity but rather because of the interference of politics in military affairs."[127] The elimination of politics within military affairs allows for the omnipotence of aggression.

To adapt to the circumstances in Vietnam, particularly that involving chasing enemy soldiers along the many inland waterways that perforated the country, the U.S. Navy revived a brown-water operation that employed converted pleasure boats, reconfigured landing craft from the Second World War, and eventually custom-built small craft as riverine combat vessels.[128] These efforts were combined with the establishment of a Mobile Riverine Force "to go after the Viet Cong in the remote reaches of the Mekong Delta and other waterways."[129] What makes this development particularly noteworthy rests with the realization – first observed from impromptu aerial surveillance – that the communist guerrillas employed expertly camouflaged vessels to secret weapons and other military assets deep into South Vietnamese territory.[130] In comparison with Latin American TCOs trafficking narcotics out of Colombia, the primary difference between the threats rests with the direction of travel.

Drug organizations secreting narcotics and other contraband *out* of South America followed the same procedures as the Viet Cong and other guerrillas smuggling weapons and personnel *into* South Vietnam.

Reflection.

In considering the aspects of law and diplomacy in war, the two cases mentioned above illustrate fundamental points pursuant to the study of narcotics smuggling via subsea vessels. First, the United States bears both the right and the precedence for attacking threats far beyond the borders of the United States. As with the Plains Indians campaigns of the 19th century, the belligerents may seek refuge across international borders, but the United States *will* seek them out and target them nevertheless. Such a policy rests within the precedence of the U.S. Diplomatic Security and Terrorism Act of 1986 that addresses terrorist acts abroad against Americans, as well as the Reagan Administration's bombing of Benghazi and Tripoli in 1985 and President Clinton's ordering of the destruction of Iraqi intelligence facilities in Baghdad during 1993.[131] Furthermore, in a strange twist of logic, the U.S. could, conceivably, employ the June 27, 1986 opinion of the International Court of Justice regarding U.S. mining of Nicaraguan harbors to its advantage in addition to the dissention of Judge Schwebel.[132] In this regard, the DTOs become perpetrators of "mining" U.S. harbors and territory through illicit narcotics.

Secondly, as experienced within Vietnam during the 20th century, a full 100 years after the conflict against native Indians, enemies of the United States may seek temporary refuge or tactical advantage in escaping across international borders. The South Asian communists operated within Laos and Cambodia to escape the tactics and presence of U.S. forces despite including them as a primary target of choice. Such tactics bear parallel to gangsters in 1930's America crossing state lines to escape prosecution. Furthermore, as Gross implies, if wealthier nations possess a moral obligation to cross national boundaries to aid and protect weaker countries, then the same argument could be made regarding crossing international borders to safeguard its citizens and to apprehend or punish malefactors.[133] Frequently, during the Plains conflicts, American troops passed into Mexico (with the approval of the Mexican government) to track marauding tribes. Such a policy parallels Colombia, which has often sought or benefitted from cooperation with the United States.[134]

Finally, in accordance with just war doctrine, the trafficking of narcotics represents a clear and present danger to the international community where silence of action represents a fundamental crime in and of itself. If international troops – in the guise of the United Nations – could not cease *genocide* within Rwanda, it remains probable that international organizations working cooperatively may not be able to cease drug trafficking out of Colombia.[135] Furthermore, Lichtenwald et al remark that SPSS vessels "have been identified setting to sea from the west coast of Colombia (Buenaventura)" as well as being "set to sea from Ecuador".[136] This indicates that the DTOs operating the subsea vessels bear no appreciation of national sovereignties, highlighting their opposition to international law and order. These observations provide substance to any unilateral U.S. declarations against trafficking organizations wherever they reside.

Other nations, notably Israel in its targeting of the perpetrators of the 1972 Munich Olympics attack, have aggressively targeted individuals from criminal/terrorist groups with little lasting international condemnation.[137] In defense of the Israeli position, political theorist Stephen de Wijze writes, "Israel faces insurmountable difficulties that prevent the arrest and trial of [terrorist individuals]."[138] Furthermore, he concludes, "[a] government's prime duty is to protect its citizens from harm, and if [targeted killing] is the only way to eliminate an imminent and serious danger, the extrajudicial killing is not just morally justified but a *moral obligation* [emphasis added]."[139] A recent ruling by the Israeli Supreme Court found that the use of targeted killing "does not automatically violate international law and its legality…must be evaluated on an individual basis" as opposed to "a set of strict criteria."[140] This opinion skirts the anti-assassination provisions of the Hague Convention and falls neatly into line with the U.S. Terrorist Elimination Act of 2001, authorizing the CIA to hunt down and kill key terrorist subjects.[141]

Few nations, therefore, remain willing to criticize other members of the international community for fear that their own interests will not be served should they find themselves needing to target specific individuals. With 175 SPSS-style drug transits during 2001 and 2010 originating in South America for global destinations, most nations perceive the dire threat from illicit subsea vessels.[142] Brian Wilson outlines the case:

> Transporting products to more profitable destinations without detection is key, and transnational criminal organizations (TCOs) operating in South America recognize the value of the oceans as critical routes, given the anonymity a ship enjoys over large, ungoverned stretches of space, the relative complexities in jurisdiction, and the limited capacity of most countries' coastal law enforcement.[143]

Moreover, the maritime security specialist hints at a commonsense solution:

> *Stopping vessels before they get underway is certainly preferable* [emphasis added], but because the construction and deployment of SPSS platforms occur in rough, rural, and isolated terrain, doing so is not always possible. This is, in part, due to the fact that smugglers are "constantly adapting their techniques to counter U.S. law enforcement activities." Consequently, identifying and tracking illicit vessels on millions of nautical miles of ocean space poses multiple operational challenges...[144]

This study suggests that the problems of "rough, rural, and isolated terrain" need not be prohibitive and that the United States military bears all the assets, personnel, training, and experience required to defeat illicit subsea vessels before they enter the vast open sea and remain vulnerable within the Colombian (and surrounding) littoral environment. All that remains required is that the United States exercises the *will* to proceed accordingly.

Narcotics Interdiction: Past, Present, and Future.

Initially, the United States chose a 'wait and apprehend' approach to drug trafficking targeting America. The law enforcement emphasis of this approach demanded the expertise of criminal investigators, whose knowledge of interpersonal relationships, finance and banking, psychology, communication skills, and foreign relations often served little but to apprehend those who sold or consumed narcotics locally.[145] When drugs received the attention of the public during the 1980s, it was either through first lady Nancy Reagan's simple "Just say no" anti-drug campaign or the romanticism of television shows such as *Miami Vice*. This somewhat lackadaisical approach to narcotics trafficking began to change when drug production and distribution emerged as a financial tool of choice for both transnational criminal organizations and terrorist groups. In the words of former U.S. Attorney General, John Ashcroft, "Terrorism and drugs go together like rats and the bubonic plague."[146]

Fishel and Manwaring contend, "[a]s long as the narco-traffickers – or any other illicit challengers – are not isolated, the credibility of their activities in a targeted country becomes greater and their legitimacy becomes stronger relative to that of the government."[147] This remains an important observation to analyze. The successful targeting and killing of Pablo Escobar in the 1990s occurred because the actions of the Colombian police Search Bloc and the paramilitary group *Los Pepes* (People persecuted by Pablo Escobar) isolated the trafficking 'kingpin'.[148] With escalating violence, Escobar drew himself into a corner and his actions became less credible amongst Colombia as a whole, further alienating him from the public and leading to more exposure to the Search Bloc. The subsequent decentralization of the narcotics traffickers, however, leading to the move away from identifiable cartels, prohibits the isolation of significant groups by Colombian and American counternarcotics operations. Yet, the U.S. approach to targeting DTOs has changed little, leading to insignificant reductions in narcotics reaching America.

What Is Not Currently Working.

The U.S. approach to countering Colombian DTOs can best be described as a part-time, law enforcement effort to engage militarily within asymmetrical warfare. Prior to the September 11, 2001 (9/11) attacks in Washington and New York, the "United States focused its money, training, and attention almost entirely on the counterdrug campaign" while for "…forty years the various Colombian governments dealt with the problem on an ad hoc basis."[149] Following the 9/11 attacks, the George W. Bush Administration "shifted its focus from one exclusively on drugs to one that addresses the problem of the narco-insurgent-paramilitary nexus."[150] Nevertheless, the precise strategy – as culled from open sources – suggests an inability to isolate the DTOs, which is magnified by the decision to begin shipping cocaine and other contraband via subsea vessels. The DTOs apparently realize that it remains exceptionally difficult to isolate vessels operating within the three-dimensional aspect of the oceans. A more significant part of the problem rests with the manner in which the U.S. and Colombia target the DTOs operating within Latin America or international waters between the two nations.

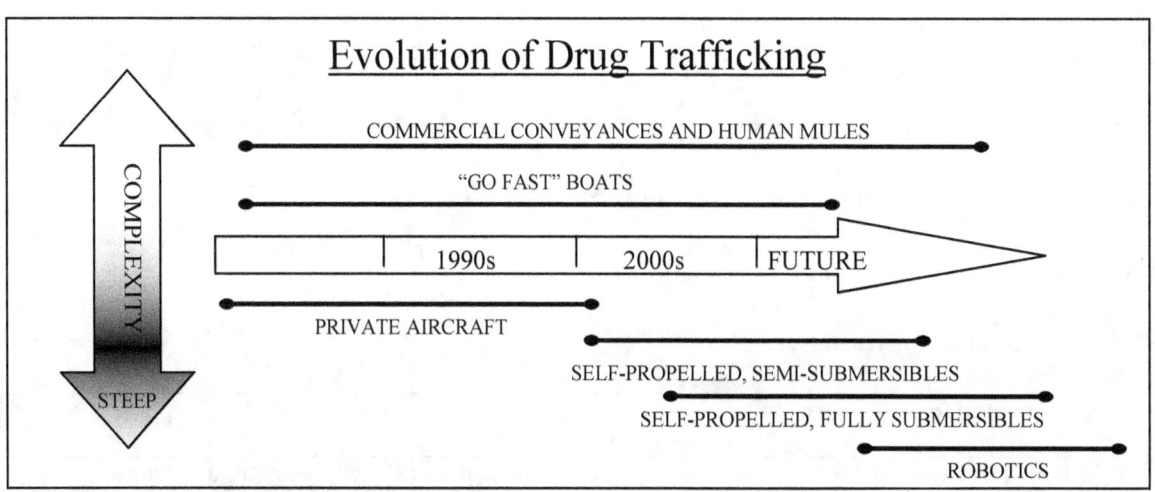

Figure 2. Progression of Trafficking Technologies.

Initially, as DTOs employed private aircraft within their smuggling operations, the United States developed the Air Bridge Denial (ABD) program to force down trafficking aircraft so that arrest and seizure could safely take place.[151] The ABD remains sufficiently successful enough to lead one incarcerated smuggler to quip, "Planes are history, because there is more surveillance now."[152] Accepted at face value, this statement corresponds with DTO smuggling activity shifting from the aerial to the subsea environments. Unfortunately, this shift in *modus operandi* granted the smuggling organizations asymmetrical advantage, largely forestalling U.S. capabilities to respond in kind. Dunigan et al suggest a bit of deception in relation to the number of SPSSs seized by the Colombian Navy (61 captures since the 1990s), that perhaps an alternative interpretation of the actual number of subsea vessels being put to sea dilutes the success of the Colombians.[153] Further criticism comes from understanding U.S. operations in Colombia.

Whenever U.S. soldiers or law enforcement personnel enter into a foreign location to act even only as advisors, their presence constitutes a literal shock to indigenous personnel, as if extraterrestrial aliens were to descend upon heartland America. Part of this problem rests with the United States military's fascination with network-centric soldiers and a myriad of electronic devices ostensibly designed to make that soldier's efforts more efficient and convenient. For instance, one potential advancement in U.S. soldiery rests with the "Tactical Assault Light Operator Suit, or TALOS, [which] is an advanced infantry uniform that promises to provide superhuman strength with greater ballistic protection."[154] This prospect further extends identification of American soldiers from those guerrillas, insurgents, and terrorists that populate fourth-generation (4GW) warfare, leading to potential resentment by more primitive, local populations.

Table 2. Four Generations of Warfare.

Evolution of Warfare	Characteristics
First-Generation	Based upon use of smooth-bore muskets, battles consisting of well-defined lines arrayed against one another in a largely open field of conflict. Example: Napoleonic Wars of 18th century.
Second-Generation	Based upon attacks against large concentrations of soldiers with maximum force. Example: World War II.
Third-Generation	Based upon maneuvers to bypass opponent's strength to target strategic assets in lieu of seeking 'body count' casualties. Example: German 'storm troopers' during WWI and blitzkrieg during WWII.
Fourth-Generation	Based upon martial, religious, economic, and political actions simultaneously.

Tactically feasible or not, such advancements in uniforms and how U.S. soldiers operate remain at odds with the requirements to target narcotics personnel and trafficking technologies within Colombia's littoral jungles. As one theorist of 4GW writes, "...no glitzy repacking of the same old 2GW [second-generation warfare] format will be good enough."[155] The modern American use of body armor, Dupont™ Kevlar® helmets, night vision optics, and other "glitzy repacking" of the soldier's uniform serves two distinct – and ill advised – functions (see Figures 3 and 4). First, it removes the individual soldier from the ability to adapt to, and merge with, the battlefield terrain. Second, it diminishes that individual soldier's confidence and ability to conduct combat operations within that particular terrain. Neither of these bode well for future evolutions of the battlefield. Furthermore, the saturation of communications in connection with such advancements serves little beyond bureaucratizing infantry divisions. Poole declares that post-Second World War American military doctrine remains "more of a policy statement than a source of warfighting procedure."[156] In other words, the "U.S. military has become so driven by 'doctrine' and 'careerism' that few of its lower ranks are willing to risk expanding upon what their manuals dictate."[157]

A second problem rests with the decibel-laden methods of transporting soldiers into combat. As within Vietnam, operations within Colombia almost exclusively focus upon the use of helicopters to insert foot soldiers into drug producing (and submarine constructing) locations. More often than not, these very same personnel are extracted by helicopter prior to sunset. This offers narco-guerrillas two opportunities to detect, by sound, the arrival of American and Colombian operatives. It also limits American counternarcotics agents from working during the nighttime hours when most indigenous guerrillas operate. To be effective, soldiers must not telegraph their capabilities and/or procedures to an enemy, lest they permit themselves to become targeted through convention and prediction. Insertion by maritime vessel – usually high-performance military/patrol boats – constitutes a similar procedure. By navigating rivers via armed patrol boats, counternarcotics forces permit themselves to be identified, cataloged, and declared suitable for potential ambush (or provide time for narcotics groups to escape).

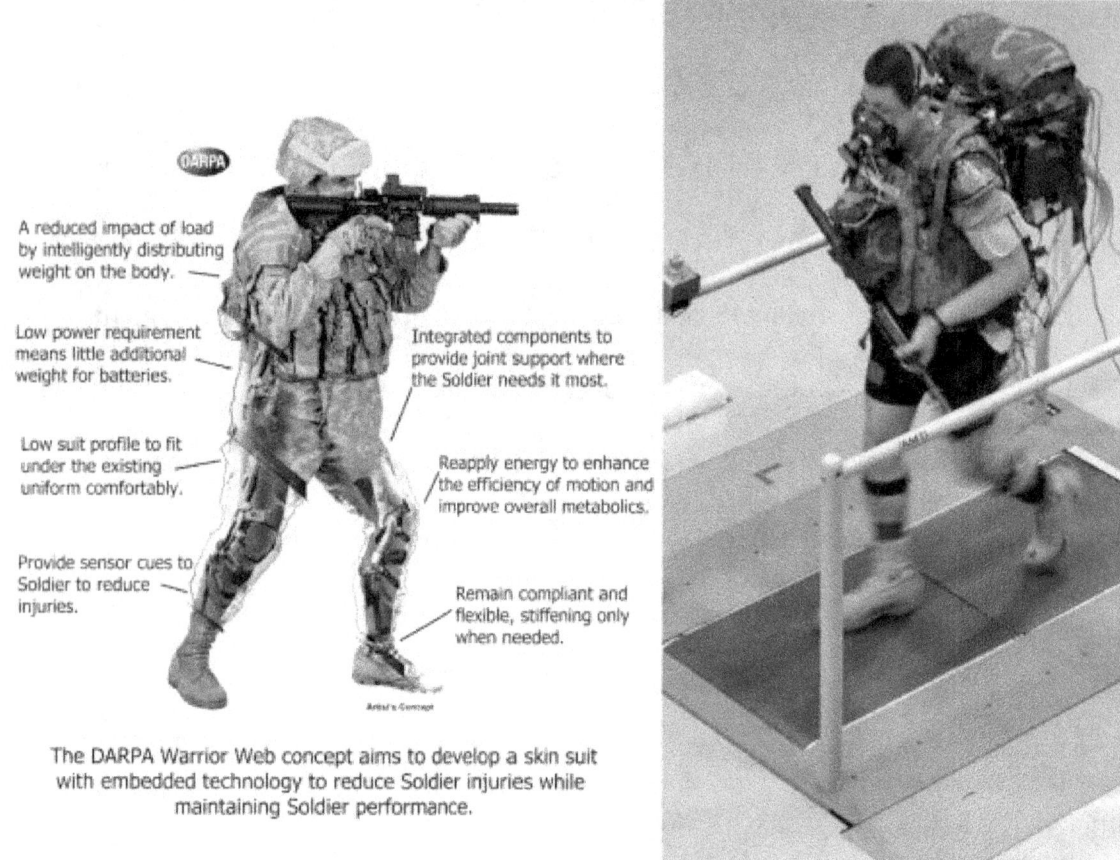

The DARPA Warrior Web concept aims to develop a skin suit with embedded technology to reduce Soldier injuries while maintaining Soldier performance.

Figure 3. DARPA Warrior Web concept

When operating within guerrilla-controlled environments, military and law enforcement professionals simply cannot allow themselves to announce their presence ahead of time. Herrington, in a personal account of fighting the Vietcong as a member of Operation Phoenix during the Vietnam War, displays eleven photographs of communist soldiers, sappers, and supporters encountered by American soldiers.[158] Every one of these individuals is dressed haphazardly, with little to distinguish him or her from the indigenous population.[159]Nevertheless, these "primitive" souls were able to confound the best-equipped and best-trained military in the world, one with virtually unlimited finances and technology at its disposal. The communist

48

Figure 4. Prospective future uniforms for the U.S. Army. www.army.mil

sappers in Vietnam, operating with a great deal of autonomy, present a lucid lesson in how to wage 4GW against illicit criminal groups such as narcotics traffickers developing advanced submarine technologies.

Burning the Military Manual and Rediscovering War.

The various DTOs and other illicit criminal organizations operating in Colombia exist to make money and will undertake *every effort* to safeguard their interests, assets, and resources whether this consists of bribing public officials, instituting social welfare programs to sway public opinion, or employing armed resistance against Colombian and American law enforcement personnel. Profit represents their ends and violence, coercion, and deceit rests as their means. In Colombia, in particular, these illicit fighters bear an acute consumption of narcotics, elevating both their aggressive tendencies and lack of remorse over their activities.[160] As with national conscript armies, the lack of professional militarism amongst the DTO foot soldiers leaves them "exceptionally vulnerable" to narcotics usage.[161] Kan reemphasizes the problem, writing:

Field Manual (FM) 3-24, the new U.S. Army field manual for counterinsurgency operations, does not include the topic of drug intoxicated combatants, even though U.S. forces continue to face them in ongoing operations. Drug use, along with drug financed warfare, is still considered to be more criminal than military in its implications and effects.[162]

This suggests that the American military leadership is not concerned with engaging warfare as an aggressive battle between two sides equipped and determined to kill individuals. Rather, the United States appears predisposed to refrain from open combat even if it means placing individuals in direct harm.

Such a disposition seems to validate criticism regarding the aforementioned advanced uniforms. What the United States apparently wants within its infantry rests a soldier completely shielded from bodily injury while seamlessly wired directly to the Pentagon and Oval Office of the White House. When he or she enters an ambush, a high-flying Predator RPV can warn the soldier of impeding crisis and unleash a Hellfire missile to target the threat without collateral damage arising from the action. If, in the extremely unlikely event that the American soldier receives injuries that cannot be handled by the dozen or so other soldiers present, then a Blackhawk helicopter flying patrol nearby will quickly land and extract the fallen individual to the nearest hospital for immediate care. Unfortunately, this scenario remains very impractical in *any* battle zone.

With an (near) instantaneous data connection to Washington – or even field headquarters – the American soldier is isolated from innovation and self-sufficiency. He will likely forestall any function if that data link is broken or headquarters does not transmit instructions rapidly enough. Secondly, the soldier may take considerable risks under the expectation of a "drone" backing them up should their limitations place them into harm's way. Thirdly, any fallen soldier amongst a group unnecessarily brings several others into the 'hot zone' that can be targeted by enemy soldiers. Watkins writes of six individuals killed by a landmine placed underneath a coca plant during an eradication mission in Colombia during November 2005.[163] How much more vulnerable would soldiers be if distracted by wounded comrades during an ambush by a hidden group? Finally, the presence of helicopters – even medevac units – offers a tempting target for guerrilla and criminal forces' antiaircraft capabilities. At a minimum, the presence of low-flying rotary wing aircraft betrays the presence of "boots on the ground".

In contrast, a guerrilla operates within his or her native ground. They learn to scour for food, use raw materials for shelter, and blend into their environment with only what nature provides. Their concept of uniform remains light and, in the case of FARC guerrillas operating in Colombia, simply consists of military-style fatigues similar to the type that Americans wore from the Second World War on through Vietnam; battle dress shirts and trousers, with minor identification markings. In Asian armies, as Poole remarks, "the distinction blurs between light infantry, special forces, and scouts."[164] This is necessarily important for it indicates that many less-technological adversaries do not segregate their commands; they employ the individualism and innovation inherent within the human species to offset shortcomings in technology. What may be "special" to American and Western armies – employing terrain appreciation, deception as a force-multiplier, individualized tactics, etc. – simply entails warfare for Eastern armies.

Thomas A. Mark's "A Model Counterinsurgency" article bears a captured photograph of a FARC sapper bearing little more than underwear briefs and a bodysuit of mud.[165] The "instructor" packing on the muck within this photograph appears to be an Asian in uniform and the caption suggests that both Cuban and Vietnamese advisors who specialize within infiltration attacks had trained FARC sappers.[166] Viewing this photograph of a lone individual covered head to toe within thick mud, one can only appreciate the 1987 movie *Predator* starring Arnold Schwarzenegger, whose character escapes the superior extraterrestrial by inadvertently covering himself with mud and thus serendipitously shielding himself from the monster's infrared vision. The lesson remains that simple, "natural" procedures can defeat even the most advanced sensor technology. An Air Force General,

Douglas Fraser, is reported to have declared, "In the mangrove swamps in Western Colombia you can be ten feet away from where somebody's building a semi-submersible and never see it."[167]

What makes this quote revealing is that it reminds one about the statement in 1962 where Army Chief of Staff George Decker declared that "any good soldier can handle guerrillas."[168] The more recent declaration simply suggests that if an Air Force general could not detect a large vessel under construction in the middle of the jungle, then, perhaps, no one else could. This, from a military and practical perspective, remains a foolish observation to make. Several thousand miles of the Ho Chi Minh Trail in Vietnam, Cambodia, and Laos remained invisible from the air, yet U.S. SOG soldiers were able to gain actionable intelligence on the road network from the ground level.[169] The statement from an air force officer, therefore, may lead counternarcotics practitioners and other government officials to conclude that infiltration efforts remain problematic when the difficulty rests with the training accorded to American soldiers. Guerrillas are, by necessity, quite adaptive and curious and would never make such a statement because they rarely possess enough workers and material to formulate complacency.

Poole supports this contention:

Guerrillas are by definition dispersed and opportunistic. Even the drug smugglers have now discovered the advantages of bottom-up organizational structure. America's only way to stop the 4GW onslaught from the south are hundreds of tiny enlisted contingents with enough skill to live among the most terrorized of the peasant populations. While perfectly logical, this is unlikely to happen – not because of any deficiency in America's youth, but because of their leaders desire to remain indispensable.[170]

We can now ascertain a more practical approach to countering DTO semi-submersibles and submarines through targeting their support and operational networks. Whether this remains a paradigm shift in American military theory or simply represents a return to historical concepts of warfare rests for the individual to decide. The assumption made, however, that the purpose of war – even if only a battle against illicit narcotics – is to:

1. Destroy an adversary's ability to wage conflict;

2. Destroy an adversary's will to commit aggression;

3. Convert former adversaries into peaceable citizens.[171]

With these conditions in mind, we can determine an appropriate response to narcotics trafficking via illicit subsea craft – destroy the DTOs ability to produce smuggling vessels, destroy the DTOs desire to invest within such technologies, and convert as many members of the support network into peaceful Colombian citizens. This study focuses upon the first two, deferring to the U.S. Department of State (DOS) and the Government of Colombia (GOC) to consider the third option.

Destroying Colombian DTOs' Ability and Desire for Subsea Trafficking.

Colombian drug organizations remain in the business of illicit narcotics trafficking solely for the profit potential of their trade. That is, at heart, anyone engaged within narcotics operations functions within a capitalistic enterprise – albeit one that remains illegal through most national laws and international treaties. To defeat them and reduce their 'business' requires either that they lose product, staff, customers, finances, or equipment. The United States and Colombia have already made significant inroads into reducing 'product' by various eradication programs, yet these emerge as impractical for the long term as indigenous coca farmers will not shy away from their illicit crops until either the U.S. or GOC provide them with an alternative. Reduction of consumption within the U.S. has been ongoing since the 'war against drugs' began, with minimalist results. Likewise, U.S. agencies such as the Department of Treasury ("Treasury") manage to isolate illicit funds on occasion, but the innovation of DTO laundering techniques keeps the narcotics groups a step ahead of Treasury investigations.

Figure 5. SPSS/SPFS Operational Hot Zones. Base image courtesy NOAA.

Therefore, the remaining DTO assets – product, staff, and equipment – must be addressed despite that these resources often appear within other counternarcotics efforts such as targeting coca fields and laboratories (product) or arrest of smugglers and producers (staff). Targeting of SPSS and SPFS networks, contrarily, requires a greater appreciation of both equipment and personnel. Subsea vessels are only vulnerable during periods of construction/launching or docking/arrival. Once out within the open sea, they remain virtually undetectable and, accordingly, free to roam (see Figure 5). Because of the vastness of the oceanic realm, the most advantageous strategy against illicit subsea vessels remains to target them (and their support/operational personnel) prior to their leaving the confines of the Colombian jungle for open water. This critical juncture matches their greatest level of vulnerability and maximizes the potential for U.S. success in defeating them.

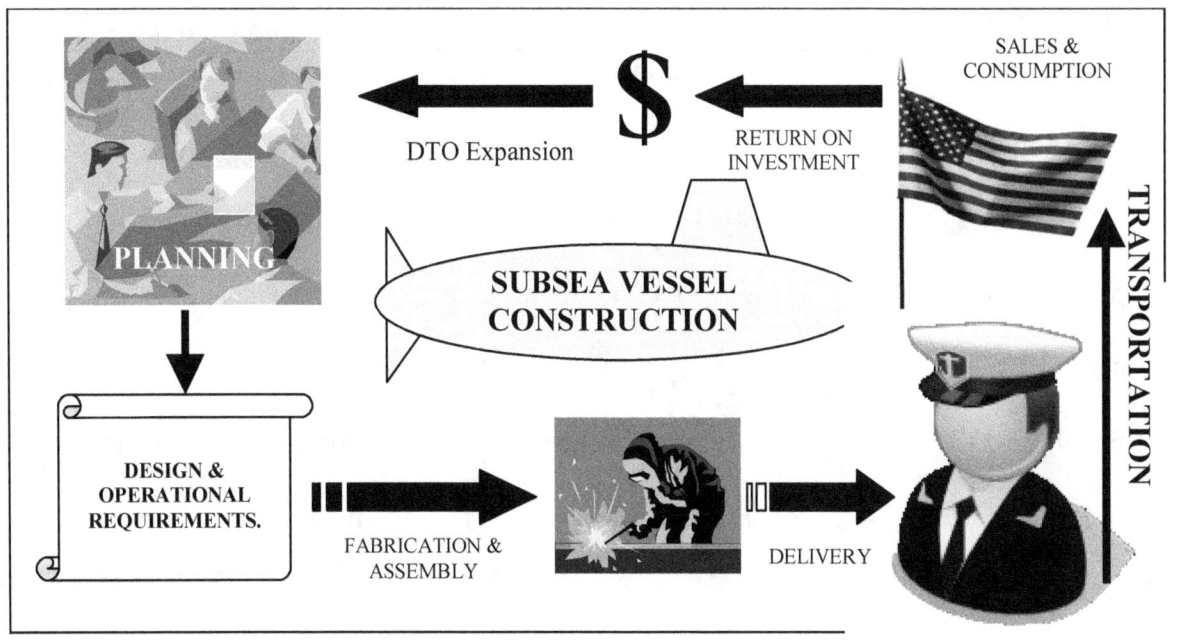

Figure 6. Facets of SPSS Construction and Operation.

The design and construction of any vessel – particularly one enveloped within illicit activity – remains a complicated process, involving dozens to potentially hundreds of individuals employed within the financial, design, engineering, construction, and maritime industries not to mention security and intimidation. To target any one individual, therefore, requires a strong human intelligence (HUMINT) capability, one capable of ascertaining the value and position of a number of people exposed to SPSS/SPFS design, development, and operation. Once their functions are determined, it becomes possible, then, to target these HVTs for neutralization.[172] Unfortunately, the U.S. HUMINT capability has not improved very much since the 1960s; where yesterday's xenophobic South Vietnamese emerges as today's equally xenophobic Colombian national.[173] To complicate matters, instead of befriending indigenous populations, Poole declares that "Western 'liberators' traditionally punish the population" leading to greater hostility towards Americans.[174] The *only* individuals that Americans should be targeting remain the critical HVTs supporting the existence of SPSS and SPFS fleets.

Financial	Construction	Operational
Investors	Engineers	Captains
Money Launderers	Naval Architects	Navigators
Illicit Bankers	Propulsion Engineers	Onboard Security
Equipment Suppliers	Equipment Installers	Trainers
Hawala-type Couriers	Site Planners	Maintenance Technicians
Stock Brokers	Advanced Welders	Support Vessel Operators
Attorneys	Foreign Advisors	Intelligence Personnel

Table 3. Potential HVTs.

Unfortunately, many nations around the world remain indiscriminate within "targeted killing" operations, leading defense analyst Thomas B. Hunter to specifically address the issue of when such targeted killing fails, including several key examples such as the Israeli operation in Lillehammer, Norway and numerous Israeli Air Force mishaps.[175] These problems – attributed solely to faulty intelligence and targeting – unnecessarily remove targeted killing options away from those culprits whose ideology, finances, or aggressiveness preclude any chance of apprehension. In fact, narcotics organizations have warned American police officers in Arizona to "look the other way" and threatened to shoot off-duty (and, apparently, any plainclothes officers the cartels deem appropriate) individuals from across the Mexican border should they interfere with smuggling operations.[176] By any consideration of international law, such efforts amount to a direct declaration of open hostilities against Americans.

Discreet targeting of HVTs employed within the design, construction, and operation of illicit subsea vehicles, however, can dismantle the social networks required to field trafficking vessels and related technologies. While 'anyone' may fill a particular need if required, certain individuals through their experience, training, position, timing, and charisma remain far more essential than anyone else.

These individuals remain rare and are often replaced by a series of people sharing various distributed duties.[177] While this does not extinguish the original function, it does dilute its efficiency as more people are employed to conduct the business of a previous single, dynamic individual. This disruption need not be massive to siphon away at DTO profits; even a minimalist interference – if conducted as part of a long-term, consistent program – would seriously hamper future trafficking programs, especially if operated in conjunction with current operations such as drug prevention and treatment, countering illicit finance activities, and apprehension and conviction. American counternarcotics efforts must go on the offensive, however, to prevent the DTOs and allied enterprises from gaining the upper hand.

Figure 7. Illicit Subsea Vessel Network Relationships.

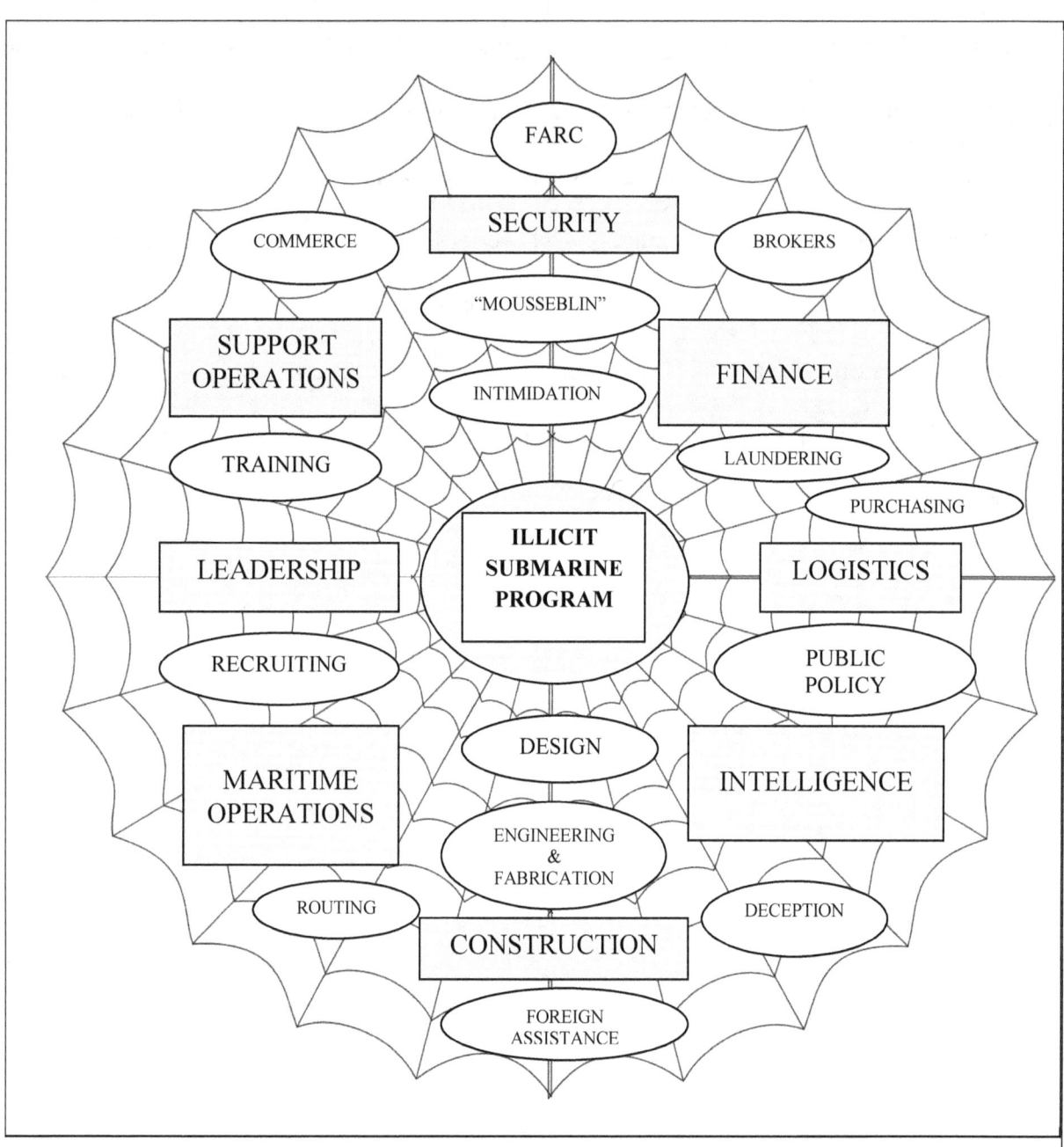

Deep-Penetration Maritime Irregular Warfare Units Engaged Against DTOs.

Clausewitz, by far the most studied Western military theorist, offers an early warning within

his book *On War* – "…war is such a dangerous business that the mistakes which come from kindness

are the very worst."[178] Others as Poole argue that such 2GW attributes needlessly alienate indigenous

populations and, therefore, the U.S. must learn to sway peasants by thinking (and, presumably, acting)

like peasants.[179] This study concludes, to the contrary, that it remains entirely possible to render kindness to indigenous populations while simultaneously thrusting fear into the hearts and minds of those whose own brutality deserves little recognition from peaceable nations. To adopt this approach, the United States must learn to "out insurgency, the insurgents". In other words, the United States must address the so-called war on drugs as it would any direct threat from a foreign invader. This remains problematic largely because of the funds earned by drug trafficking that foster corruption at best and a unilateral arms race at worst. Nevertheless, the United States must shift its policies in order to address what amounts to the most diabolical enemy ever encountered by American soldiers.

At this point, several key assumptions require addressing. First, there remains a general acceptance of the United States to engage within targeted killing, even if only from Hellfire missiles launched by Predator RPVs. Hunter acknowledges, "It is clear that targeted killing has become an accepted foreign policy option, with a tacit rationale in self-defence."[180] This suggests that targeting by missile should not dissuade the U.S. from targeting with individuals, particularly in view of the killing of Osama bin Laden. Second, even social networks bear a targetable node that represents a vulnerability to the whole organization. Williams identifies these nodes as "network cores" and each bears "asymmetries of power, influence, and status" in relationship to the periphery of the network.[181] Third, no indigenous population will ever consider itself 100% loyal to American interests and will, therefore, likely represent an impediment to U.S. missions during the course of operations. Herrington offers an analogy:

> The American role in Vietnam reminded me of the proud father who bought his three-year-old son an electric train. When the son proved to be too young to operate the complex toy, the father had taken it over and run it himself. Months later, the son still couldn't run the train because the father became so wrapped up in the toy that he never bothered to teach the boy...For several years, American units had fought the war and given little more than lip service to training the Vietnamese to "run the train".[182]

In Colombia, America must turn local soldiers into 'locomotive engineers' while still acknowledging that the locals may be corrupt, inefficient, traitorous, or otherwise incapable of mounting an effective attack against DTO groups.[183] Fortunately, the employment of large tactical

units, such as the DEA and other military forces currently utilize, is not very efficient for countering

DTO submarine construction sites and social networks. Poole endorses small, two to three man CAP

units operating across the drug trafficking regions with the civilian population serving as an

instrumental element of the CAP's security apparatus.[184] Regardless, these small – and very numerous

– CAP units serve well within the deep jungle, but along the riverine environment they pose certain

infiltration and extraction problems (it previously noted that helicopters and small patrol craft remain

loud, cumbersome, and impractical in matters of utmost secrecy). This study proposes a completely

new approach to embedding Poole's CAP units into the riverine jungle harboring DTO submarine

construction sites.

Novelist Frederick Forsyth, author of the *Dogs of War*, envisioned the use of a small cargo

vessel to launch his mercenary attack from the sea.[185] This remains a tactically viable option as the

planet remains populated with nondescript cargo vessels of all sizes and shapes, including many

examples that cost less than some of the soldier's weapon systems employed by the United States'

equipment-saddled infantry.[186] Such vessels would deploy American troops aboard quiet, inflatable

boats that could enter Colombia's many waterways under the cover of darkness or inclement weather

and escape unnecessary scrutiny for their casual, commercial appearance. Combined with, perhaps, a

conventional helicopter insertion of Colombian and American DEA agents west of the SPSS

construction sites that could provide a diversion of FARC guerrillas for clandestinely infiltrating CAP

units from seaward. The small units, operating with a degree of autonomy from the bureaucracy in

Washington, would find themselves in an effective position to harass DTO forces while still engaging

cooperation from the local population.

Consisting of culturally appreciative soldiers – e.g., Spanish speakers of Latin American

heritage – combined with a Colombian national or two, the proposed CAP teams could operate

undetected within a specific region for a given period. To multiple their efforts – and survival –
however, these CAP units would don FARC-style uniforms and carry indigenous (e.g., AKMS/AK-47
Kalashnikov weapons) firearms. This "false flag" approach will serve to shield American involvement
and permit the United States a great deal of deniability. The employment of twelve, four-man CAP
teams encompassing 48 soldiers can, conceivably, patrol the entire southwestern coast of Colombia,
maximizing their surveillance on those principal regions where SPSS activity is probable and
occasionally surveying the remainder of their operational radius to gather intelligence regarding
guerrilla activity as may be necessary. With deployments of up to six months in duration, these CAP,
or Hunter-Killer (HKT) teams, could operate far more effectively than DEA teams that require
extraction by sunset on any given day.

What would make these HKTs survivable rests upon their ability to intermingle with the
indigenous peoples and exhibit a degree of microterrain appreciation sufficient to escape detection by
and confrontation with enemy guerrillas.[187] These teams would not "arrive" as much as would current
DEA investigations as the individuals would, apparently, always be "there" in the view of most
transient personnel (those that have not noticed their presence beforehand will likely assume that they
migrated over from a neighboring village or urban center). To anticipate each HKT's effectiveness, the
"relative superiority" concept envisioned by McRaven must be considered.[188] This theory rests upon
determination of the achievement of relative superiority gained against an adversary based upon key
events experienced during missions evolving from point of vulnerability (PV) on through mission
completion and is measured in hours from the

Figure 8. Hunter-Killer Team (HKT) Deployments.

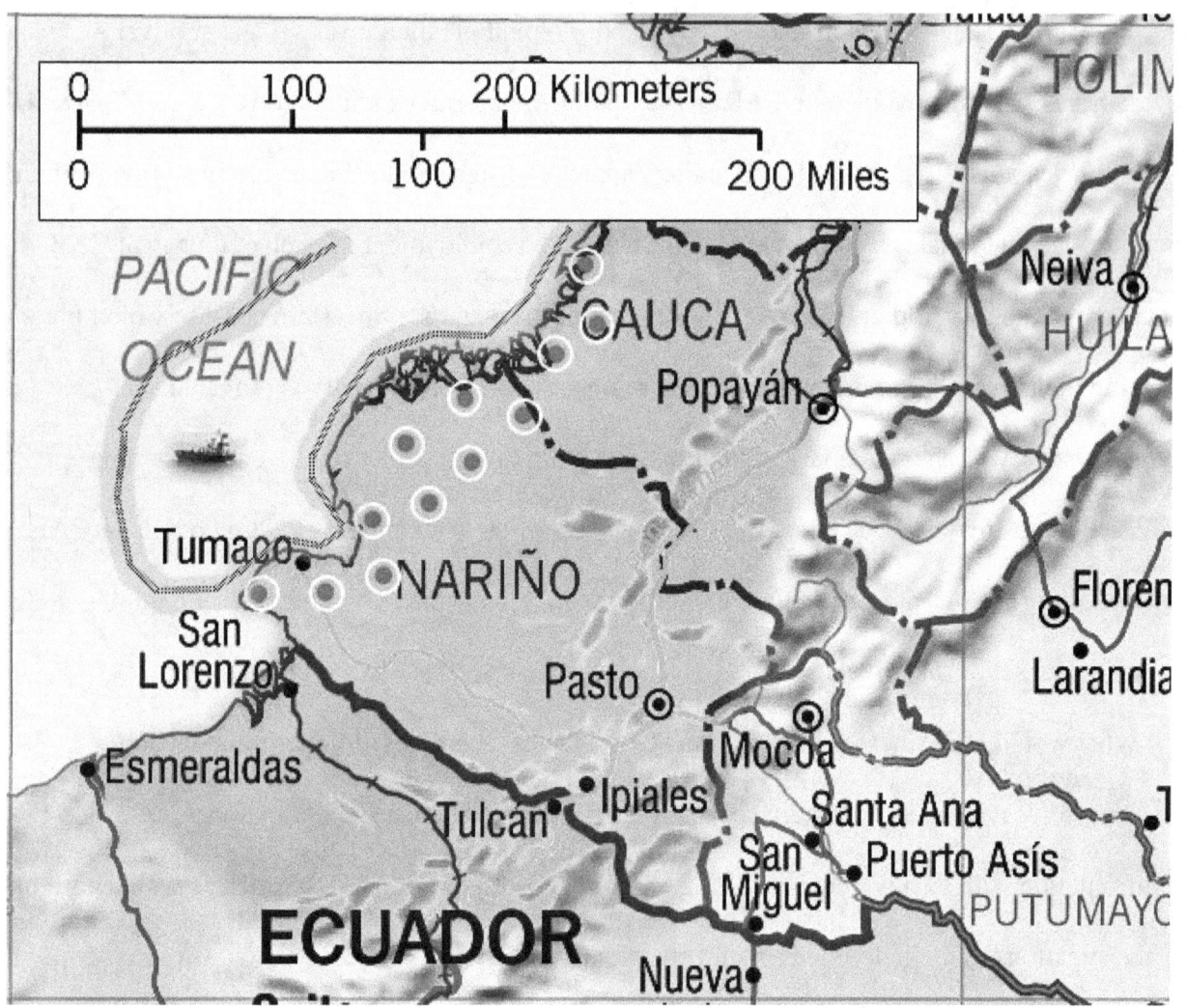

start of the particular mission in question.[189] More pragmatically, HKT missions must be considered in

light of the six principles of special operations identified by McRaven: simplicity, security, repetition

(in preparation, training, etc.), surprise, speed, and purpose.[190]

With these qualifiers in mind, it remains possible to consider this study's HKT concept in

comparison with other active counternarcotics efforts employed by the United States, including social

drug prevention and treatment programs, U.S. Coast Guard (USCG) Helicopter Interdiction Tactical

Squadron (HITRON) interdiction,[191] DEA/GOC excursions into DTO territory, and international

diplomacy. When proposing a new approach to any endeavor, however, it remains complicated to

envision various effects beforehand. With this in mind, this study attempts to eliminate such

problematic conditions with generic expectations of each category and hypothesis. That is, examination of each category will remain under empirical consideration based upon the consulted sources already identified within this research. From here, discussion will follow to clarify any ambiguities associated with the study's hypotheses.

Table 4. Consideration of Five Options for Dealing with DTO Submarines.

QUALIFIER	TREATMENT	HITRON	DEA/GOC	DIPLOMACY	HKT
SIMPLICITY	X			X	X
SECURITY		X			X
REPETITION	X	X	X	X	X
SURPRISE					X
SPEED		X			X
PURPOSE	X	X	X	X	X

From the above, only USCG and proposed HKT operations score highly on a significant number of qualifiers. The proposed HKT units diminish a bit on speed (once on location, the teams will not be able to quickly move to other locations) and purpose (their function expires with no targetable HVTs). Otherwise, the concept scores effectively in simplicity, security, repetition, and surprise. The appearance of tiny, indigenous teams right in the heart of DTO locations with minimal connection to bureaucracy assures these units of surprise and security, something that helicopter-borne or diplomatic alternatives do not provide. HITRON operations, which the United States has invested a great deal of time, effort, and funding within, fail in surprise (again, helicopters do not appear without telegraphing their arrival) and simplicity – which often involves several nearby vessels and air traffic control issues. Furthermore, multimillion-dollar rotary- and fixed-wing aircraft could fund dozens of HKT operations for a great many years. The conclusion rests that onsite, autonomous hunter-killer teams present the most effective case for dismantling SPSS and SPFS construction programs.

V. CONCLUSION.

Whether considered as 'cartels' or simply defined as an obscure collection of social networks, organizations engaged within the subsea trafficking of narcotics and other illicit goods represent the pinnacle of criminality, one that ignores the existence of national boundaries and international law and order. More substantial than Islamic jihadists, more adaptable than nation-state adversaries, and far more deadly than any other non-state actor, drug trafficking organizations, as but a minor field of transnational criminal organizations, represent a clear and present danger to American national security interests. Their ability to corrupt through bribery, evade through coercion and murder, and ply their trade through unmatched profits and technological innovation assures these organizations of longevity and resilience. They cannot be defeated through bureaucracy, diplomacy, or feebleness. Any group of individuals that explodes commercial airliners, beheads as a means of intimidation, and threatens U.S. law enforcement from across borders will not, in the advice of Clausewitz, be swayed by kindness.

Present U.S. strategies remain burdened by bureaucracy and military tradition. Failing to diminish the American consumption of narcotics, the U.S. has opted for a strategy of interdiction and eradication. When American counternarcotics agents do participate within preemptive missions, it usually involves some manner of accompanying Colombian military/law enforcement personnel into the jungle via helicopter or patrol vessel insertion. Such methods, unfortunately, telegraph their arrival through sound, preparation, and complexity of purpose. More often than not, such missions are extracted before sunset to increase the safety of participating members. Accordingly, the U.S. places severe limitations upon the actions of its operatives, sacrificing efficiency for international courtesy and personal expectations. Meanwhile, the trafficking organizations remain free to rule their territory to the exclusion of legitimate public authority and evolve their smuggling technologies at will.

To defeat these criminal organizations, the U.S. must abandon concepts of law enforcement, apprehension, and view subsea vessels as dedicated weapons of war (unlike private aircraft that have been modified for illicit purposes). Semi-submersibles, submarines, and, most recently, autonomous robotic vehicles remained designed for a singular purpose: to circumvent international navies and aircraft in order to smuggle contraband throughout the world. Any vessel capable of carrying tons of cocaine, for instance, remains quite capable of transporting other prohibited items such as biological, chemical, and nuclear devices.[192] Furthermore, such vessels bear an immediate capacity to carry human cargoes such as slaves, transnational criminals, and infiltrating terrorists.[193] The potential targeting of a U.S. harbor could unleash more damage upon the American economy than the September 11, 2001 attacks in Washington and New York caused. The United States must, therefore, add teeth to its verbal declarations of war. It must conclude that the criminal elements building and operating the submarines have violated all expectations of legal consideration and have forfeited Geneva considerations accorded to uniformed army personnel.[194]

Interdiction upon the open ocean may appear legal – in consideration of the U.S. Drug Trafficking Vessel Interdiction Act of 2008 – yet laws only hold value if they remain obeyed. By definition, such legislation represents merely a form of "post event" response action where the apprehended suffer the consequences of indigenous politics. In war, laws are necessarily broken and the conditions outlined within this study suggest that 'just law' provisions remain applicable. Therefore, the United States retains the right to engage within direct targeting of DTO personnel, especially those individuals whose functions bear the direct responsibility for circumventing international diplomacy and national sovereignty. Targeted killing represents "the one truly effective countermeasure that is able to combat [terrorism and narco-trafficking]."[195] Unfortunately, American concepts of targeted killing often involve standoff weapons designed to be dropped or fired from thousands of feet in the air. Such actions breed more collateral deaths than perhaps any other aggressive action taken by the United States.

To dismantle illicit submarine networks, the U.S. must fully engage within the HUMINT opportunities offered by such avenues as building forces up from within indigenous communities. Invasion by mass represents the surest way in which to aggravate normally xenophobic cultures.

Penetrating local communities sends a ripple effect throughout an entire region, earning the alertness of DTO intelligence apparatuses. To reduce this eventuality, U.S. efforts must clandestinely embark personnel from the sea so that airports, bus terminals, and other prominent public facilities do not register the arrival of foreigners. Furthermore, the presence of one or a few individuals in remote locations does not attract as much attention as do the presence of large groups of uniformed personnel boarding Blackhawk helicopters for locations that criminal elements could only imagine. More covert approaches to Colombia shield American operations from tainted Colombian law enforcement agencies under the influence of drug smugglers, adding an additional level of secrecy to counternarcotics operations.

This study highlights a distinction of counternarcotics operations engaged against drug trafficking organizations employing advance subsea technologies to affect their trade. On the one hand, rests current U.S. practices of interdiction, eradication, and apprehension. This approach represents a human-intensive, technology-driven mission where fleets of ships and aircraft feint an impenetrable barrier against foreign invasion. When a limited number of subsea craft are detected, these forces quickly move in to apprehend the crews and cargos before these vessels can be scuttled. In Colombia, the U.S. – largely through DEA agents – works hand-in-hand with the Colombian National Police (CNP) to recruit informants to gain knowledge about suspected cocaine submarines and processing laboratories. When located, these facilities are ordinarily destroyed by teams inserted by helicopters or patrol craft. American soldiers accompanying these forces bear a distinguishable appearance of "U.S." using M-4 assault rifles, body armor, Kevlar® helmets, encrypted communications, night vision optics, and even sometimes *National Geographic* television crews. Most of these missions remain terminated by the constraints of helicopter support.

In contrast, the hypothesized approach of this study incorporates the lessons learned over two hundred years of American experiences, ranging from the exploits of Maj. Robert Rogers of pre-revolutionary society on through the Chindits of World War II and SOG soldiers in Vietnam. This approach literally fights fire with fire as U.S. HKT soldiers condition themselves to act and think much like the Asian soldiers advising the FARC guerrillas. Instead of arriving by noisy helicopters, these tiny contingents are offloaded by seemingly decrepit cargo vessels sailing close to the southwestern coast of Colombia, not far away from Tumaco. Employing inflatable boats powered by muffled outboard engines, the four-man contingent slowly navigates into the riverine environment, preferably under the cover of inclement weather, at night to quickly build hides from which they shall conduct their missions. Each team will consist of two-man elements so that one-half of the HKT can sleep or eat while the other pair provides security and observation.

These American soldiers are not uniformed like conventional grunts. They have dispensed with most of the technologies accorded to U.S. soldiers and more resemble their pre-WWII brethren than the special operations soldiers spending months and years refining their craft. These 'new' soldiers represent light infantry warriors whose training was measured in weeks; their fundamental training taking a page from the Selous Scouts of Rhodesia – "the fledgling [HKT members] had to live off the land for 18 days" before being assigned to Colombian counter-submarine duties.[196] Bureaucracy and doctrine do not constrict their innovation and ability to adapt. In fact, looking, acting, and thinking like American soldiers represents a death sentence for these troops as they arrive wearing local guerrilla uniforms pursuant to the FARC rebels guarding cartel submarine construction sites. Nor do they ever communicate within the English language or bear modern, Western-preferred weapons. Each soldier's greatest asset rests with his ability to escape detection.

Once onshore, the HKT teams would move inland, hugging the terrain and avoiding producing silhouettes against bright surfaces. By avoiding the enemy, they would allow themselves to represent phantom soldiers, sabotaging DTO assets when found and leaving evidence of competitive drug groups to divert scrutiny from American forces. When locating HVTs or other targets of opportunity, as identified via previous intelligence, they will neutralize the threat in accordance with the best method possible. One more engineer, financier, boat captain, or guerrilla leader will cease benefitting the DTOs and no one will attach the defection, retirement, or death to a tiny band of American soldiers spanning the Colombian coast. Six months after arriving on scene, the tiny detachments will begin to motor back out to sea under the cover of darkness to rendezvous with another innocuous cargo vessel sailing between North and South America.

The research has shown that the United States certainly bears the ability to wage war against the Colombian DTOs and, perhaps, even the desire to convert these enemies into honorable members of society. Unfortunately, it has become apparent that Washington does not bear the *will* to defeat the DTOs and their clandestine submarine building networks. As with most wars of the past, the U.S. appears more conducive to waging indiscriminate conflicts where some successes are achieved to offset any number of collateral casualties. Yet, to target specific individuals to terminate their refusal to abandon criminal and terroristic practices seems foreign to American leadership. A Hellfire missile fired from afar appears much more tolerable than a series of innovative and aggressive soldiers "already there". Without "unconditional victory" against the drug traffickers, America will never win the battles against emerging technologies until, perhaps, a SPSS or SPFS leads to the destruction of a major city or two. Then, the U.S. may decide to begin sending tiny hunter-killer units on missions of vengeance, but such would merely represent a bandage against a gaping wound…

VI. GLOSSARY OF TERMS.

Asymmetrical Warfare: Conflict involving a disparity between sides in arms, moral propensity, economic prevalence, technology, and/or tactical prowess.

***Bloque de Búsqueda* (Search Bloc)**: Colombia special police unit involved in the tracking and killing of Pablo Escobar during the early 1990s.

Combined Action Platoon (CAP): A small military unit consisting of U.S.-led indigenous forces.

Cartel: Illicit narcotics transnational criminal organization, often used with the name of the city or region representing the base of operations (e.g., Cali cartel, Medellín cartel, Mexican cartels, etc.).

Centra Spike. Covert U.S. military special operations unit assigned to aid Colombia in the targeting of Pablo Escobar.

CDL: Clandestine Drug Laboratory.

Delta Force: Elite U.S. Counterterrorism response unit.

DTO: Drug Trafficking Organization.

False Flag: Any operation, military or political in origin, that seeks to disguise its participants' allegiance.

FARC: *Fuerzas Armadas Revolucionarias de Colombia.* Leftist guerrilla group in Colombia. Splinter groups espouse both Marxist and Maoist doctrine.

Fourth-Generation Warfare (4GW): "Warfare in four arenas simultaneously – martial, religious, economic, political."[197]

Guerrilla: A member of, or a collective group representing, irregular warfare units combating established military and/or state political and law enforcement agencies usually employing armed aggression.

HUMINT: Human intelligence.

IED: Improvised Explosive Device, any of a series of "homemade" explosive devices or military explosive devices improvised for secondary uses beyond their design capacity.

MIW: Maritime Irregular Warfare.

PLA/PLAN: People's Liberation Army (Chinese military forces)/People's Liberation Army Navy.

PRC: People's Republic of China.

SOF: Special operations forces.

SPFS: Self-Propelled Fully Submersible. Maritime vessel that completely submerges beneath the water with no structural features rising above the surface for extended periods.

SPSS: Self-Propelled Semi-Submersible. Maritime vessel that can submerge only partially, usually with a conning tower or some other aspect of the vessel's hull showing above water.

Targeted Killing: The specific targeting of an *individual*, isolated through intense HUMINT investigation, for killing as a means to affect some measure of military/security advantage while reducing collateral damage to civilian populations.

Ungoverned Spaces: Territories largely outside the control of legitimate political authority and/or governance.

VII. ENDNOTES.

[1] Ronald Reagan: "Radio Address to the Nation on Federal Drug Policy," October 2, 1982. Online by Gerhard Peters and John T. Woolley, *The American Presidency Project*. http://www.presidency.ucsb.edu/ws/?pid=43085.

[2] Mark Bowden, *Killing Pablo: The Hunt for the World's Greatest Outlaw* (New York: Penguin Books, 2001), 29.

[3] Kim Cragin and Bruce Hoffman, *Arms Trafficking and Colombia* (Santa Monica, CA: RAND Corporation, 2003), 4.

[4] Lance J. Watkins, *Self-Propelled Semi-Submersibles: The Next Great Threat to Regional Security and Stability*, Thesis (Monterey, CA: Naval Postgraduate School, 2011), 26-35.

[5] Ibid.

[6] Ibid., *iii*.

[7] Robert Spalding, *Drug Subs: The Worldwide Invasion by the Narco-Submarine Fleet* (Signal Mountain, TN: Spalding Publishing, 2010), 45-67.

[8] Molly Dunigan, Dick Hoffman, Peter Chalk, Brian Nichiporuk, and Paul Deluca, *Characterizing and Exploring the Implications of Maritime Irregular Warfare* (Santa Monica, CA: RAND Corporation, 2012), 42-48.

[9] H. John Poole, *Tequila Junction: 4th-Generation Counterinsurgency* (Emerald Isle, NC: Posterity Press, 2008), 181.

[10] Michael L. Gross, *Moral Dilemmas of Modern War: Torture, Assassination, and Blackmail in an Age of Asymmetric Conflict* (New York: Cambridge University Press, 2010), 233-252.

[11] Poole, *Tequila Junction*, 169.

[12] Gregory D. Lee, *Global Drug Enforcement: Practical Investigative Techniques* (Boca Raton, FL: CRC Press, 2004), 34.

[13] Hugh Thomas, *Conquest: Montezuma, Cortés, and the Fall of Old Mexico* (New York: Simon and Schuster, 1993), 487.

[14] Paul Rexton Kan, *Drug Intoxicated Irregular Fighters: Complications, Dangers, and Responses* (Carlisle, PA: Strategic Studies Institute, March 2008), 4.

[15] Ibid., 11.

[16] Ibid., Endnote 26.

[17] Phil Williams and Vanda Felbab-Brown, *Drug Trafficking, Violence, and Instability* (Carlisle, PA: Strategic Studies Institute, April 2012), 8.

[18] Dunigan, Hoffman, Chalk, Nichiporuk, and Deluca, *Maritime Irregular Warfare*, 43.

[19] Spalding, *Drug Subs*, 18-25.

[20] See http://dealbook.nytimes.com/2012/12/10/hsbc-said-to-near-1-9-billion-settlement-over-money-laundering/ (accessed May 2013). See also http://www.americancriminallawreview.com/Drupal/blogs/blog-entry/hsbc-and-money-laundering-%E2%80%9Ctoo-big-indict%E2%80%9D-02-15-2013 (accessed May 2013).

[21] Rachel Ehrenfeld, Funding Evil: How Terrorism is Financed – and How to Stop It (Chicago: Bonus Books, 2003), 146.

[22] Ibid., 158-166.

[23] Michael Kenney, *From Pablo to Osama: Trafficking and Terrorist Networks, Government Bureaucracies, and Competitive Adaptation* (University Park, PA: The Pennsylvania State University Press, 2007), 25-47.

[24] John Marks, *The Search for the "Manchurian Candidate": The CIA and Mind Control* (New York: Times Books, 1979), 122. Gordon Thomas, *Journey into Madness: The True Story of Secret CIA Mind Control and Medical Abuse* (New York: Bantam Books, 1989), 264-265.

[25] *America's Book of Secrets*, "The Drug Wars", Season 2, Episode 8, [Originally aired May 24, 2013]. This program provides a substantial indictment of the CIA's involvement within cocaine smuggling from Latin America to the United States and, perhaps far worse, Justice Department participation within the illicit arms trade in Latin America.

[26] Scott H. Decker and Margaret Townsend Chapman, *Drug Smugglers on Drug Smuggling: Lessons from the Inside* (Philadelphia: Temple University Press, 2008), 69-87.

[27] Ibid.

[28] R. Evan Ellis, *China-Latin America Military Engagement: Good Will, Good Business, and Strategic Position* (Carlisle, PA: Strategic Studies Institute, August 2011), 2-9.

[29] H. John Poole, *Dragon Days: Time for "Unconventional Tactics"* (Emerald Isle, NC: Posterity Press, 2007), 21-22.

[30] Kenney, *From Pablo to Osama*, 63.

[31] Decker and Chapman, *Drug Smugglers*, 34-35.

[32] John P. Sullivan and Adam Elkus, "Narco-Armor in Mexico", *Small Wars Journal* (July14, 2011). www.smallwarsjournal.com.

[33] Ann Marie Brodarick, "High Sea, High Stakes: Jurisdiction over Stateless Vessels and an Excess of Congressional Power Under the Drug Trafficking Vessel Interdiction Act" *University of Miami Law Review* 67 (2012): 255-256.

[34] Ibid., 265.

[35] Watkins, *Self-Propelled*, 35.

[36] U.S. Congress. *Drug Trafficking Vessel Interdiction Act of 2008*. 11th Congress, 2nd Session, 2008. S.3598.

[37] Brodarick, "High Seas, High Stakes", 257-258.

[38] Michael L. Gross, *Moral Dilemmas of Modern War: Torture, Assassination, and Blackmail in an Age of Asymmetric Conflict* (New York: Cambridge University Press, 2010), 21-25.

[39] W. Michael Reisman and Chris T. Antoniou, *The Laws of War: A Comprehensive Collection of Primary Documents on International Laws Governing Armed Conflict* (New York: Vintage Books, 1994), 84-86.

[40] Philip Gourevitch, *We wish to inform you that tomorrow we will be killed with our families: Stories from Rwanda* (New York: Picador, 1998), 114.

[41] Harry G. Summers, Jr. *On Strategy: A Critical Analysis of the Vietnam War* (New York: Presidio Press, 1982), 73. Paul Balor, *Manual of the Mercenary Soldier* (Boulder: Paladin Press, 1988), 77.

[42] Poole, *Tequila Junction*, 169-172.

[43] William H. McRaven, *SPEC OPS: Case Studies in Special Operations Warfare: Theory and Practice* (New York: Presidio Press, 1995), 1-25.

[44] Ibid., 8.

[45] Robert G. Spulak, Jr., *A Theory of Special Operations: The Origin, Qualities, and Use of SOF* (Hurlburt Field, FL: Joint Special Operations University, October 2007), *vii*.

[46] Ibid., 14-15.

[47] Scott Wimberley, *Special Forces Guerrilla Warfare Manual* (Boulder: Paladin Press, 1997), 35-114.

[48] Thomas J. Cutler, *Brown Water, Black Berets* (Annapolis, MD: Naval Institute Press, 1988), 137.

[49] Ibid., 162.

[50] Larry Chambers, *RECONDO: LRRPs in the 101st Airborne* (New York: Ballantine Books, 1992), 1-17.

[51] Michael Lee Lanning, *Inside the LRRPs: Rangers in Vietnam* (New York: Presidio Press, 2006), 80-81. Of particular interest rests the discussion of William Gawthrop, this researcher's former professor from AMU course INTL 414.

[52] Paul Balor, *Manual of the Mercenary Soldier* (Boulder: Paladin Press, 1988), 22.

[53] Mao Tse-tung, *On Guerrilla Warfare* (New York: Classic House Books, 2009), 2-9.

[54] Ernesto "Che" Guevara, *Guerrilla Warfare* (n.l.: BN Publishing, 2007), 7-11.

[55] Carlos Marighella, *Mini-Manual of the Urban Guerrilla* (n.d., booklet ostensibly printed by the Black Panthers and/or The Weathermen terrorist groups ~ Wisconsin circa 1970), 6.

[56] Robert Taber, *War of the Flea: The Classic Study of Guerrilla Warfare* (Dulles, VA: Potomac Books, 2002), 1-16.

[57] Paladin Press, *Handbook for Volunteers of the Irish Republican Army* (Boulder: Paladin Press, 1985), 5-7.

[58] H. John Poole, *The Tiger's Way: A U.S. Private's Best Chance for Survival* (Emerald Isle: Posterity Press, 2003), 38.

[59] Graham H. Turbiville, Jr. *Guerrilla Counterintelligence: Insurgent Approaches to Neutralizing Adversary Intelligence Operations* (Hurlburt Field, FL: Joint Special Operations University, January 2009), 44.

[60] Poole, *Tiger's Way*, 94-95.

[61] Scott Swanson, "Know Your Enemy: Human Intelligence Key to SOF Missions", *Special Warfare* (January-February 2007): 18.

[62] William S. Lind, Keith Nightengale, John F. Schmitt, Joseph W. Sutton, and Gary I. Wilson, "The Changing Face of War: Into the Fourth Generation" in *Global Insurgency and the Future of Armed Conflict* eds. Terry Terriff, Aaron Karp, and Regina Karp (New York: Routledge, 2008), 19.

[63] Ibid., 20.

[64] Robert M. Clark, *Intelligence Analysis: A Target-Centric Approach, Second Edition* (Washington: CQ Press, 2007), 31.

[65] Kenney, *From Pablo to Osama*, 51-77.

[66] Scott Swanson, "Viral Targeting of the IED Social Network System", *Small Wars Journal* 8 (May 2007), 9.

[67] Aram Roston, "Update: SOUTHCOM ISR helped kill 'narco-terrorists', *C4ISR Journal* (June 2013): 8.

[68] Ibid.

[69] Bowden, *Killing Pablo*, 72-78.

[70] Phil Williams, "Transnational Criminal Networks" in *Networks and Netwars: The Future of Terror, Crime, and Militancy* eds. John Arquilla and David Ronfeldt (Santa Monica, CA: RAND Corporation, 2001), 64.

[71] Ibid., 65.

[72] Ibid., 71.

[73] Decker and Chapman, *Drug Smugglers*, 34.

[74] Michael Kenney, "The Architecture of Drug Trafficking: Network Forms of Organization in the Colombian Cocaine Trade" *Global Crime* 8, no. 3 (August 2007): 233.

[75] Swanson, "Viral Targeting", 4.

[76] Watkins, *Self-Propelled*, 27.

[77] Ibid.

[78] Kenney, *From Pablo to Osama*, 104.

[79] Ibid., 104.

[80] Decker and Chapman, *Drug Smugglers*, 69.

[81] Ibid., 207, notes for Chapter Seven, *n2*.

[82] Watkins, *Self-Propelled*, 30.

[83] Dunigan, Hoffman, Chalk, Nichiporuk, and Deluca, *Maritime Irregular Warfare*, 45.

[84] Ibid., 46.

[85] Spalding, *Drug Subs*, 56-57.

[86] Marco de Andreis and Francesco Calogero, *The Soviet Nuclear Weapon Legacy* (New York: Oxford University Press, 1995), 47.

[87] Watkins, *Self-Propelled*, 3.

[88] W. Alejandro Sanchez, "Russia and Latin America at the Dawn of the Twenty-First Century", *Journal of Transatlantic Studies* 8, no. 4 (December 2010): 363-364.

[89] Ibid., 373.

[90] Ibid., 369.

[91] Ibid.

[92] Cragin and Hoffman, *Arms Trafficking*, 28.

[93] Sanchez, "Russia and Latin America", 369.

[94] Watkins, *Self-Propelled*, 9.

[95] Turbiville, *Guerrilla Counterintelligence*, 43-44.

[96] Enrique Desmond Arias, "Understanding Criminal Networks, Political Order, and Politics in Latin America" in *Ungoverned Spaces: Alternatives to State Authority in an Era of Softened Sovereignty* eds. Anne L. Clunan and Harold A. Trinkunas (Stanford, CA: Stanford University Press, 2010), 115.

[97] R. Evan Ellis, *China-Latin America Military Engagement: Good Will, Good Business, and Strategic Position* (Carlisle, PA: Strategic Studies Institute, August 2011), 31.

[98] Ibid.

[99] Ibid. 25.

[100] Ellis, *China-Latin America*, 32-33.

[101] Mao, *Guerilla Warfare*, 38.

[102] Bowden, *Killing Pablo*, 27.

[103] Poole, *Tequila Junction*, 3.

[104] Bowden, *Killing Pablo*, 81.

[105] Ibid.

[106] Poole, *Tequila Junction*, 172.

[107] John F. Ross, *War on the Run*: *The Epic Story of Robert Rogers and the Conquest of America's First Frontier* (New York: Bantam Books, 2009). 452.

[108] Ibid., 461-466.

[109] John L. Plaster, *SOG: The Secret Wars of America's Commandos in Vietnam* (New York: NAL Caliber, 1997), 26.

[110] Dick Couch, *A Tactical Ethic: Moral Conduct in the Insurgent Battlespace* (Annapolis, MD: Naval Institute Press, 2010), *xv*.

[111] Ibid., *xiii-xiv*.

[112] Gross, *Moral Dilemmas*, 126-127.

[113] George W. Grayson, *La Familia Drug Cartel: Implications for U.S.-Mexican Security* (Carlisle, PA: Strategic Studies Institute, December 2010), 1.

[114] Gross, *Moral Dilemmas*, 21.

[115] Thomas Goodrich, *Scalp Dance: Indian Warfare on the High Plains, 1865-1879* (Mechanicsburg, PA: Stackpole Books, 1997), 8.

[116] Ibid., 148-149.

[117] Robert L. Utley, "Crooks and Miles, Fighting and Feuding on the Indian Frontier", *MHQ: The Quarterly Journal of Military History* 2, no. 1 (1989): 90.

[118] Goodrich, *Scalp Dance*, 13.

[119] United States Catholic Conference, Inc., *Catechism of the Catholic Church* (New York: Doubleday, 1994), Paragraph # 2309.

[120] Ibid., #2291.

[121] Ibid., #2265.

[122] Summers, *On Strategy*, xiii.

[123] John L. Plaster, *Secret Commandos: Behind Enemy Lines with the Elite Warriors of SOG* (New York: Simon and Schuster, 2004), 314-315.

[124] Ibid., 232.

[125] Summers, *On Strategy*, 21.

[126] Ibid.

[127] Mao, *Guerrilla Warfare*, 18.

[128] Ken Olsen, "'Just Plain Sexy'", *The American Legion Magazine* (July 2013), 20-26.

[129] Ibid., 24.

[130] Cutler, *Brown Water*, 76-77.

[131] Reisman and Antoniou, *Laws of War*, 315-316.

[132] Ibid., 12-18.

[133] Gross, *Moral Dilemmas*, 219.

[134] Bowden, *Killing Pablo*, 43.

[135] Gourevitch, *We wish to inform*, 114.

[136] Lichtenwald, Steinhour, and Perri, "Maritime Threat Assessment", 3-4.

[137] Aaron J. Klein, *Striking Back: The 1972 Munich Olympics Massacre and Israel's Deadly Response* (New York: Random House, 2005), 97-103.

[138] Stephen de Wijze, "Targeted Killing: a 'Dirty Hands' Analysis", *Contemporary Politics* 15, no. 3 (2009): 313.

[139] Ibid.

[140] Ibid., 306.

[141] Ibid., 307.

[142] Brian Wilson, "Submersibles and Transnational Criminal Organizations", *Ocean and Coastal Law Journal* 17, no. 1 (2011): 36.

[143] Ibid., 39.

[144] Ibid., 40.

[145] Lee, *Global Drug Enforcement*, 4-5.

[146] Ehrenfeld, *Funding Evil*, 3.

[147] John T. Fishel and Max G. Manwaring, *Uncomfortable Wars Revisited* (Norman, OK: University of Oklahoma Press, 2006), 194-195.

[148] Bowden, *Killing Pablo*, 179-180.

[149] Fishel and Manwaring, *Uncomfortable Wars*, 240.

[150] Ibid.

[151] Watkins, *Self-Propelled*, 16.

[152] Decker and Chapman, *Drug Smugglers*, 80.

[153] Dunigan, Hoffman, Chalk, Nichiporuk, and Deluca, *Maritime Irregular Warfare*, 46-47.

[154] Roger Teel, "Army explores futuristic uniform for SOCOM", U.S. Army Research, Development and Engineering Command Public Affairs, May 28, 2013. http://www.army.mil/article/104229/ Accessed June 20, 2013.

[155] Poole, *Tequila Junction*, 192.

[156] Ibid., 175.

[157] Ibid.

[158] Stuart A. Herrington, *Stalking the Vietcong: Inside Operation Phoenix: A Personal Account* (New York: Ballantine Books, 1982), photo insert between pages 104-105.

[159] Ibid.

[160] Kan, "Drug Intoxicated", 4.

[161] Ibid., 24.

[162] Ibid., 26.

[163] Watkins, *Semi-Submersibles*, 14.

[164] Poole, *Tiger's Way*, 9.

[165] Thomas A. Marks, "A Model Counterinsurgency: Uribe's Colombia (2002-2006) vs FARC" in *Military Review* (March-April 2007): 42.

[166] Ibid.

[167] Watkins, *Semi-Submersibles*, 23.

[168] Summers, *On Strategy*, 73.

[169] Plaster, *SOG*, 34.

[170] Poole, *Tequila Junction*, 189.

[171] R.J. Godlewski, "Latte Intelligence: The Divorce of Shock Creativity and Special Information Operations" *American Intelligence Journal* 29, no. 1 (2011): 70.

[172] Herrington, *Stalking the Vietcong*, 17. In this context, "neutralization" includes coercion to defect, employment as an informant, capture, and/or killing.

[173] Ibid.

[174] Poole, *Tequila Junction*, 182.

[175] Thomas B. Hunter, *Targeted Killing: Self-Defense, Preemption, and the War on Terrorism* (Lexington, KY: BookSurge, 2009), 61-70.

[176] Mark Spicer, "Mexican Drug Cartels: The Growing Threat of the Sniper Attack" *Journal of Counterterrorism & Homeland Security International* 16, no. 4 (2011): 49.

[177] Kenney, *From Pablo to Osama*, 45-46.

[178] Carl von Clausewitz, *On War*, eds. and trans. Michael Howard and Peter Paret (Princeton, NJ: Princeton University Press, 1976), 75.

[179] Poole, *Tequila Junction*, 182.

[180] Hunter, *Targeted Killing*, 40.

[181] Williams, "Transnational Criminal Networks", 72.

[182] Herrington, *Stalking the Vietcong*, 22.

[183] Bowden, *Killing Pablo*, 172-173.

[184] Poole, *Tequila Junction*, 246-249.

[185] Frederick Forsyth, "Forward" in Al J. Venter, *War Dog: Fighting Other People's Wars: The Modern Mercenary in Combat* (Drexel Hill, PA: Casemate, 2008), *xi*.

[186] For a range of specimens, see http://commercial.apolloduck.com/listings.phtml?cid=4. Accessed June 21, 2013.

[187] Poole, *Tiger's Way*, 47-56.

[188] McRaven, *SPEC OPS*, 7.

[189] Ibid.

[190] Ibid., 11-23.

[191] Watkins, *Semi-Submersibles*, 20.

[192] Ibid., 50.

[193] Spalding, *Drug Subs*, 68-70.

[194] Reisman and Antoniou, *Laws of War*, 44.

[195] Hunter, *Targeted Killing*, 48.

[196] Poole, *Tequila Junction*, 203.

[197] Ibid., 305.

VIII. BIBLIOGRAPHY.

Arias, Enrique Desmond. "Understanding Criminal Networks, Political Order, and Politics in   Latin America." In *Ungoverned Spaces: Alternatives to State Authority in an Era of   Softened Sovereignty*, edited by Anne L. Clunan and Harold A. Trinkunas, 115-135.   Stanford, CA: Stanford Security Studies/Stanford University Press, 2010.

Balor, Paul. *Manual of the Mercenary Soldier.* Boulder: Paladin Press, 1988.

Bowden, Mark. *Killing Pablo: The Hunt for the World's Greatest Outlaw.* New York: Penguin Books, 2001.

Brodarick, Ann Marie. "High Seas, High Stakes: Jurisdiction over Stateless Vessels and an Excess of Congressional Power Under the Drug Trafficking Vessel Interdiction Act." *University of Miami Law Review* 67 (2012): 255-276.

Chambers, Larry. *RECONDO: LRRPs in the 101st Airborne.* New York: Ballantine Books, 1992.

Clark, Robert M. *Intelligence Analysis: A target-centric approach.* Washington: CQ Press, 2007.

Clausewitz, Carl von. *On War.* Translated by Michael Howard and Peter Paret. Princeton: Princeton University Press, 1984.

Couch, Dick. *A Tactical Ethic: Moral Conduct in the Insurgent Battlespace.* Annapolis, MD: Naval Institute Press, 2010.

Cragin, Kim, and Bruce Hoffman. *Arms Trafficking and Colombia.* Santa Monica, CA: RAND Corporation, 2003.

Cutler, Thomas J. *Brown Water, Black Berets.* Annapolis, MD: Naval Institute Press, 1988.

De Andreis, Marco, and Francesco Calogero. *The Soviet Nuclear Weapon Legacy.* New York: SIPRI/Oxford University Press, 1995.

Decker, Scott H., and Margaret Townsend Chapman. *Drug Smugglers on Drug Smuggling: Lessons from the Inside.* Philadelphia: Temple University Press, 2008.

De Wijze, Stephen. "Targeted killing: a 'dirty hands' analysis." *Contemporary Politics* 15, no. 3 (September 2009): 305-320.

Ehrenfeld, Rachel. *Funding Evil: How Terrorism is Financed -- and How to Stop it.* Chicago: Bonus Books, 2003.

Ellis, R. Evan. *China-Latin America Military Engagement: Good Will, Good Business, and Strategic Position.* Carlisle, PA: Strategic Studies Institute, 2011.

Fishel, John T., and Max G. Manwaring. *Uncomfortable Wars Revisited.* Norman, OK: University of Oklahoma Press, 2006.

Forsyth, Frederick. "Forward." In *War Dog: Fighting Other People's Wars: The Modern Mercenary in Combat*, by Al J. Venter, vii-xii. Drexel Hill, PA: Casemate, 2008.

Godlewski, R.J. "Latte Intelligence: The Divorce of Shock Creativity and Special Information Operations." *American Intelligence Journal* 29, no. 1 (2011): 70-79.

Goodrich, Thomas. *Scalp Dance: Indian Warfare on the High Plains 1865-1879.* Mechanicsburg, Pennsylvania: Stackpole Books, 1997.

Gourevitch, Philip. *We wish to inform you that tomorrow we will be killed with our families.* New York: Picador, 1998.

Grayson, George W. *La Familia Drug Cartel: Implications for U.S.-Mexican Security.* Carlisle, PA: Strategic Studies Institute, 2010.

Gross, Michael L. *Moral Dilemmas of Modern War: Torture, Assassination, and Blackmail in an Age of Asymmetric Conflict.* New York: Cambridge University Press, 2010.

Guevara, Ernesto. *Guerrilla Warfare.* BN Publishing, 2007.

Herrington, Stuart A. *Stalking the Vietcong: Inside Operation Phoenix: A Personal Account.* New York: Ballantine Books, 1982.

Hunter, Thomas B. *Targeted Killing: Self-Defense, Preemption, and the War on Terrorism.* Lexington, KY: BookSurge, 2009.

Kan, Paul Rexton. *Drug Intoxicated Irregular Fighters: Complications, Dangers, and Responses.* Carlisle, PA: Strategic Studies Institute, 2008.

Kenney, Michael. *From Pablo to Osama: Trafficking and Terrorist Networks, Government Bureaucracies, and Competitive Adaptation.* University Park, PA: The Pennsylvania State University Press, 2007.

Kenney, Michael. "The Architecture of Drug Trafficking: Network Forms of Organisation in the Colombian Cocaine Trade." *Global Crime* 8, no. 3 (August 2007): 233-259.

Klein, Aaron J. *Striking Back: The 1972 Munich Olympics Massacre and Israel's Deadly Response.* New York: Random House, 2007.

Lanning, Michael Lee. *Inside the LRRPs: Rangers in Vietnam.* New York: Presidio Press, 2006.

Lee, Gregory D. *Global Drug Enforcement: Practical Investigative Techniques.* Boca Raton, FL: CRC Press, 2004.

Lichetenwald, Terrance G., Mara H. Steinhour, and Frank S. Perri. "A Maritime Threat Assessment of Sea Based Criminal Organizations and Terrorist Operations." *Homeland Security Affairs* 8, no. 13 (August 2012): 1-24.

Lind, Wiliam S., Keith Nightengale, John F. Schmitt, Joseph W. Sutton, and Gary I. Wilson. "The Changing Face of War: Into the Fourth Generation." In *Global Insurgency and the Future of*

Armed Conflict, edited by Terry Terriff, Karp, Aaron and Regina Karp, 13-20.   New York: Routledge, 2008.

Marighella, Carlos. *Mini-Manual of the Urban Guerrilla.*

Marks, John. *The Search for the "Manchurian Candidate": The CIA and Mind Control.* New York: Times Books, 1979.

Marks, Thomas A. "A Model Counterinsurgency: Uribe's Colombia (2002-2006) vs FARC." *Military Review*, March-April 2007: 41-56.

McRaven, William H. *SPEC OPS: Case Studies in Special Operations Warfare: Theory and Practice.* New York: Ballantine Books, 1996.

Olsen, Ken. "'Just Plain Sexy'." *The American Legion Magazine*, July 2013: 20-25.

Paladin Press. *Handbook for Volunteers of the Irish Republican Army.* Boulder, CO: Paladin Press, 1985.

Plaster, John L. *Secret Commandos: Behind Enemy Lines with the Elite Warriors of SOG.* New York: Simon and Schuster, 2004.

—. *SOG: The Secret Wars of America's Commandos in Vietnam.* New York: NAL Caliber, 1997.

Poole, H. John. *Dragon Days: Time for "Unconventional" Tactics.* Emerald Isle, NC: Posterity Press, 2007.

—. *Tequila Junction: 4th-Generation Counterinsurgency.* Emerald Isle, NC: Posterity Press, 2008.

—. *The Tiger's Way: A U.S. Private's Best Chance for Survival.* Emerald Isle, NC: Posterity Press, 2003.

Reisman, W. Michael, and Chris T. Antoniou. *The Laws of War: A comprehensive collection of primary documents on international laws governing armed conflict.* New York: Random House, 1994.

Ross, John F. *War on the Run: The Epic Story of Robert Rogers and the Conquest of America's   First Frontier.* New York: Bantam Books, 2009.

Roston, Aram. "Update: SOUTHCOM ISR helped kill 'narco-terrorists'." *C4ISR Journal*, June 2013: 8.

Sanchez, W. Alejandro. "Russia and Latin America at the Dawn of the Twenty-First Century." *Journal of Transatlantic Studies* 8, no. 4 (December 2010): 362-384.

Spalding, Robert. *Drug Subs: The Worldwide Invasion by the Narco-Submarine Fleet.* Signal Mountain, TN: Spalding Publishing, 2010.

Spicer, Mark. "Mexican Drug Cartels: The Growing Threat of the Sniper Attack." *Journal of Counterterrorism & Homeland Security International* 16, no. 4 (2011): 48-50.

Spulak Jr., Robert G. *A Theory of Special Operations: The Origin, Qualities, and Use of SOF.* JSOU Report 07-7, Hurlburt Field: Joint Special Operations University, 2007.

Sullivan, John P., and Adam Elkus. "Narco-Armor in Mexico." *Small Wars Journal*, July 2011.

Summers Jr, Harry G. *On Strategy: A Critical Analysis of the Vietnam War.* New York: Presidio Press, 1982.

Swanson, Scott. "Viral Targeting of the IED Social Network System." *Small Wars Journal*, May 2007: 2-16.

—. "Know Your Enemy: Human Intelligence Key to SOF Missions." *Special Warfare*, January-February 2007: 16-24.

Taber, Robert. *War of the Flea: The Classic Study of Guerrilla Warfare.* Washington: Potomac Books, 2002.

Thomas, Gordon. *Journey into Madness: The True Story of Secret CIA Mind Control and Medical Abuse.* New York: Bantam Books, 1989.

Thomas, Hugh. *Conquest: Montezuma, Cortes, and the Fall of Old Mexico.* New York: Simon and Schuster, 1993.

Tse-tung, Mao. *On Guerrilla Warfare.* New York: Classic House Books, 2009.

Turbiville Jr., Graham H. *Guerrilla Counterintelligence: Insurgent Approaches to Neutralizing Adversary Intelligence Operations.* JSOU Report 09-1, Hurlburt Field, FL: Joint Special Operations University, 2009.

Turbiville Jr., Graham H. *Hunting Leadership Targets in Counterinsurgency and Counterterrorist Operations: Selected Perspectives and Experiences.* JSOU Report 07-6, Hurlbert Field: Joint Special Operations University, 2007.

U.S. Congress. "Drug Trafficking Vessel Interdiction Act of 2008." Washington: 110th Congress, Second Session, January 3, 2008.

United States Catholic Conference, Inc. *Catechism of the Catholic Church.* New York: Doubleday, 1994.

Utley, Robert L. "Crook and Miles, Fighting and Feuding on the Indian Frontier." *MHQ: The Quarterly Journal of Military History*, Autumn 1989: 81-91.

Watkins, Lance J. *Self-propelled Semi-submersibles: The Next Great Threat to Regional Security and Stability.* Thesis, Monterey: Naval Post-Graduate School, 2011.

Williams, Phil. "Transnational Criminal Networks." In *Networks and Netwars: The Future of Terror, Crime, and Militancy*, edited by John Arquilla and David Ronfeldt, 61-97. Santa Monica, California: RAND Corporation, 2001.

Williams, Phil, and Vanda Felbab-Brown. *Drug Trafficking, Violence, and Instability.* Carlisle, PA: Strategic Studies Institute, 2012.

Wilson, Brian. "Submersibles and Transnational Criminal Organizations." *Ocean and Coastal Law Journal*, 2011: 35-63.

Wimberley, Scott. *Special Forces Guerrilla Warfare Manual.* Boulder: Paladin Press, 1997.